DECORATIVE WOODCARVING
Accessories for the Home

DECORATIVE WOODCARVING

Accessories for the Home

FREDERICK WILBUR

GUILD OF MASTER CRAFTSMAN PUBLICATIONS LTD

First published 2008 by
Guild of Master Craftsman Publications Ltd
Castle Place, 166 High Street,
Lewes, East Sussex BN7 1XU

ISBN 978–1–86108–521–4

Photographs and drawings are by the author except on pages 1,
2, 67, 84, 106, 135, 159, which are by Ron Hurst/Photoworks
Creative Group; and the wood samples by Anthony Bailey.

Production Manager: Jim Bulley
Managing Editor: Gerrie Purcell
Editor: Mark Bentley
Managing Art Editor: Gilda Pacitti
Designer: Fineline Studios

Set in Charter

Colour origination by GMC Reprographics
Printed and bound in China by Sino Publishing

Safety

Woodcarving should not be a dangerous
activity, provided that sensible
precautions are taken to avoid
unnecessary risk.

Always ensure that work is securely held
in a suitable clamp or other device, and
that the workplace lighting is adequate.

Keep tools sharp; blunt tools are
dangerous because they require more
pressure and may behave unpredictably.
Store them so that you, and others, cannot
touch their cutting edges accidentally.

Be particular about disposing of
shavings, finishing materials, oily rags,
etc., which may be a fire hazard.

Do not work when your concentration is
impaired by drugs, alcohol or fatigue.

Do not remove safety guards from power
tools; pay attention to electrical safety.

The safety advice in this book is
intended for your guidance, but cannot
cover every eventuality: the safe use of
hand and power tools is the
responsibility of the user. If you are
unhappy with a particular technique or
procedure, do not use it – there is always
another way.

Dedication

This is dedicated to Elizabeth without whom this book and my woodcarving career would not have been possible; she is the clearing in my deep woods.

Acknowledgements

Books can be magical things and I hope this book has some inspiring projects for the amateur and advanced woodcarver, subtle as the magic might be. But there is no slight-of-hand here. Books are one of the richest wonders of the world, made from a limited range of alphabetical characters, made by combining the facts of ideas to create revolutionary action, made from much behind-the-scenes activity and yet presented to the world at face value. Every author has many assistants: the woman he saws in half, the rabbit who waits patiently for his time, the volunteer who rises from the audience; each privy to their own function. In my hope that this book has a magical quality to it, I want to thank all who have contributed to it: The most magical person I know is Elizabeth, who happens (magically) to be my wife. It is hard to say more.

I want to thank the following people who have seen value in publishing my words: John Lavine, Editor of Woodwork, and Ross Periodicals for information originally published in issue #39. Stuart Lawson of GMC Publications for information originally published in Woodcarving #60, #62, #83, #87. Alan Giagnocavo, Publisher, and Shannon Flowers, Editor, of Fox Chapel Publishing for information originally published in Woodcarving Illustrated #32, #35, and #40.

There are others who have permitted me to use their material: John Grafton of Dover Publications, Inc. for permission to use illustrations contained in several of their publications. I also want to thank Anita Ellis, deputy director of curatorial affairs, and Amy Miller Dehan, curator of decorative arts of the Cincinnati Art Museum, for introducing me to the Cincinnati art-carvers, and the museum for permission to use photographs of pieces from the collection.

Contents

"The forcible writer stands behind his words with his experience."

Henry David Thoreau *Journal* March 18, 1842.

Chapter One

Inspirations

◆ **Aspects of craft** ◆ **Efficient woodcarving**

Between smartly carved bookends, among the Renaissance treatises of Alberti and Palladio, the ornamental histories and commentaries of Owen Jones, Ruskin and Pugin, is a dog-eared copy of *Manual of Traditional Wood Carving*, its cover faded to a Victorian shade of lavender.

Originally published in 1910 at the dénouement of woodcarving's glory days, it is the definitive work on historical woodcarving as well as a practical instruction book. I purchased the Dover Publications, Inc. reprint of this work in 1977 and was immediately fascinated by the pages of photographs and drawings. I have been incessantly inspired by the book since, and it is fair to say that the study of its contents and an interest in art and architecture provoked me to choose a career in woodcarving. The inspiration for the present book derives from *Manual of Traditional Wood Carving* and other nineteenth century carving manuals and from a commitment to foster and preserve the traditional designs and practices of the decorative woodcarver.

The intention in writing this book is to present the construction and decoration by woodcarving of a variety of functional accessory items. Most contemporary woodcarving project books are fixated on technique, having reduced the artistic process into chip-by-chip photographic sequences.

Often they pedantically and superficially include chapters on tools and sharpening with some condescending notes on woods. There are, however, some books which do address these areas with alacrity and should be consulted. These are listed in the bibliography.

Rarely do the popular 'how-to' books mention the design considerations of the projects undertaken. With this book the four aspects of woodcarving (indeed, any craft), namely **design**, **material**, **tools** and **technique**, have been more fully integrated into the discussions of the applications. The household items presented here encompass a range of technical difficulty, but many are suitable for those modestly acquainted with woodcarving techniques. None is beyond the abilities of the serious student.

Much background has been presented in my previous books, *Carving Architectural Detail in Wood* and *Carving Classical Styles in Wood*. These books provide practical information on the purchase of tools, carving terminology, the making of a work station, the relationship of form and light, and the different variations of relief carving. There are demonstrations in these books of many techniques to produce decorated mouldings, cartouches, capitals, rosettes, voluted brackets, finials and keystones. They also provide many historical examples of architecture and ornamental detail.

The Aspects of Craft

Designs and influences

The **designs** described and carved here derive from historic sources: from actual examples in museums, private collections, historic houses, and from nineteenth century printed sources, including carving manuals. Reference to traditional carving designs is derived from that of Western culture: from Greece and Rome, through Europe, specifically England, and to America. One must be aware, however, of the Oriental influence on the West which began in earnest in the eighteenth century (Chinese Chippendale, for instance) and continued through the later nineteenth century Aesthetic Movement. The fact that these designs are derived from historical precedent does not mean that

making these projects precludes creativity or artistic influences from other cultures.

The relationship of design to object is discussed and some stylistic notes provide the background to integrate new ideas into the type of item chosen to carve. Within the functional construction of the wall pockets described in Chapter Three, for instance, there can be a myriad of possible carved designs as well as a variety of techniques used to accomplish them. The designs presented here are in the style of the later nineteenth century interpretations of the Classical, the Gothic and the Renaissance and not strict reproductions. There has been and continues to be an interest in the artistic movements of the later nineteenth century; the Aesthetic Movement, Arts and Crafts and Art Nouveau.

Those who want to research additional stylistic alternatives to those illustrated here are encouraged to consult the bibliography for guidance. Full sized, ready to use, patterns are not generally supplied here for the simple reason that preliminary drawing is necessary for visualizing and understanding the process of the carving to be done. Drawing, as will be mentioned frequently, is an essential ingredient in creating effective designs. I hope the explanations here will provide a strong basis for the reader to design and accomplish a satisfactory woodcarving.

Left **Flowing oak leaves inspired by nineteenth century design**

Opposite **Music Cabinet**

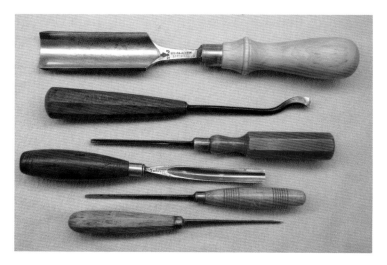

Left **Become familiar with your tools**

Materials, tools and techniques

The **material** of our craft is for the most part, of course, wood. We often work with other materials, however, such as clay and urethane foam, finishes and ancillary materials such as metal hardware. Though contemporary woodworkers are able to purchase woods from around the world, there are a limited number of species in the Anglo-American tradition, based on availability, working properties and historical context. The amateur woodcarver should not be dissuaded from trying various woods as a learning experience, but clearly there are some woods more amenable to the amateur carver. The work described here is made from indigenous North American woods with the exception of Honduran mahogany (and substituted species). The work herein described is made of black walnut (*juglans nigra*), butternut (*juglans cinerea*), cherry (*prunus serotina*), soft or red maple (*acer rubrum*), and mahogany (*swietenia mahagoni*).

One cannot explain technique without referring to **tools**. It is assumed that the reader will have a fundamental knowledge of his tools, but there will be discussion of tools in relation to the work at hand. To direct the reader to use a specific tool is problematic for several reasons: tools, even of the same designation, may differ among manufacturers, or the reader's set of gouges may lack some tool specified in the text. This is one of the problems with the prevalent step-by-step descriptions in some woodcarving periodicals. The novice must become intimately familiar with his tools, learning the interchangeable character of gouges and the carving properties of each tool. Tool types will be mentioned where appropriate.

The three aspects outlined above support and are integral with **technique**, which can be defined as the use of tools to execute a design in the material. Though one common criterion for the judging of woodcarving is technique, it is not separate from design. Nor is design estranged from technique. The four artificial divisions of design, material, tools and technique are integrated into a (hopefully) successful work of art. The techniques described here are traditional ones using the traditional tools of the carver and do not address the many possibilities of power carving which in many applications and circumstances is a legitimate alternative. Even in the traditional context one may use power tools for specific tasks such as roughly shaping a large piece of wood or routing the ground of a carving with a hand held router, or cleaning up small recessed areas with a small rotary burr.

Two Themes

Other than discussion of the four aspects of craft as outlined above, two themes will be evident throughout this book. The first will explore the design thought process; the why and how a design is created and deemed appropriate for the material, or function of the piece. Though much of traditional carving is derived from designs previously created, there are many considerations one must contemplate in order to produce an effective carving. One must think about the appropriateness of the style to the situation, the depth of relief to the function of the object, the design to the space allotted for it, the scale and proportion of the design to the overall object, and so forth. Many of these considerations may depend on the intended location of the piece (hung high on a wall, placed on a bedroom bureau or on an occasional table) and the possible lighting situation.

The second theme explores the notion that experience (practice) is truly the best teacher. All 'how-to' books are written under the assumption that we learn by imitation and having a four-year-old granddaughter constantly reminds me of this platitude. Early in my carving career I attempted to replicate items described in various carving books; the leaf exercise and the sample cuts board illustrated in Wheeler and Hayward's *Woodcarving*, a candlestick in Franz Meyers' *Handbook of Ornament* (explored in detail in Chapter Six), a tray explained in Andrew Marlow's *Fine Furniture for the Amateur Cabinetmaker*. I even copied verbatim the Italian Renaissance mantelpiece described at some length in the previously mentioned *Manual of Traditional Woodcarving*.

You should constantly self critique, comparing your work with similar examples, with accepted design principles and with your own earlier efforts. Observing historical examples will also contribute greatly to this self-analysis. With this in mind, I have reprised objects I carved in younger years to show how one's carving can be improved. One characteristic of an accomplished artisan is that learning and improving are part of the creative process.

Above **Self-critiquing led to the creation of this lamp. See page 159**

Applications

Each chapter presents several related accessories or furnishings with encompassing alternate constructions and a variety of covered designs. For instance, in Chapter Three, *Wall Pockets and Bookracks*, both types of accessory consist of flat panels which can be decorated by incised, flat or low relief carving. A total of twelve completed items are illustrated. There are occasionally ancillary photographs of examples not described by sequence photographs, such as the two older folding bookracks. Most projects require a modestly equipped shop (or access to one) for the dressing and cutting of stock, the making of simple joints and the fabrication of 'blanks'. Basic woodworking knowledge is also necessary to make the pieces accurately, to assemble them well and to finish the piece when carved. In keeping with the purpose of the book, however, primary attention is given to the carved decoration of the projects and not overly to the woodworking aspects. This is done, in part, by avoiding complex constructions, the use of specialized equipment, custom-made or hard to find hardware or sophisticated finishing techniques. The one possible exception to this is the use of a biscuit joiner, but I believe its use is widely accepted today.

Inspiration and enthusiasm often encourages us to be unrealistic about what we can actually sustain, so beginning with a project which you think you can easily do based on your personal carving history is to be recommended. It is better to work on a 'simple' carving and learn how to carve it efficiently and confidently than to take on a challenging one and be frustrated or unable to sustain the necessary effort. There is no sequential order of difficulty in the applications presented here, so you can work on what interests you.

Efficient Carving

People have expressed surprise that I make a living (such as it is) from woodcarving and at times I'm amazed myself. Recently, a young carver made the comment to me that I must be able to make a living because I carve efficiently. Although I have always striven to do so, I sometimes feel more impatient than efficient and stressed out when a commission takes me too long to finish. After his remark, I began to think about my business survival in terms of efficiency, and considered the habits and aids I had accumulated over the years. The usual notion is that the artist experiments, fools around a lot, trying to arrive at some grand statement, and that such labour-intensive activities as woodcarving don't make money these days.

Of course, there are many aspects which contribute to a viable carving business, and being able to carve efficiently certainly is one of them. The professional carver sells his skill, and the manifestation of that skill is the product. Skill is accumulated over years of practice, thorough knowledge of the woodcarving and woodworking trades, and by mastering technique. Efficiency ties together these aspects of skill.

I consider myself a trade carver, working by commission for millwork and furniture companies, architects and designers with occasional direct commissions from individuals. I am consistently held to price quotes and almost always to a time frame. To remain competitive these two factors demand efficiency (an industrious attitude, at least!) Carvers can be efficient in a number of ways. Some are based on common sense, such as having a congenial shop or studio which has adequate lighting and work area. Another is practicing orderly work habits, but there are seven specific approaches I have found helpful.

Preparedness

Before you begin to carve, draw the design full size, make a model if necessary, and prepare the blank accurately. Pictured is a drawing translated into a three dimensional

Above **The drawing translated into a three dimensional clay model and the finished carving in mahogany**

Below **Sketches of traditional ornament and from nature**

guide and a picture showing sketches of various ornament. Whether you develop the design or it is supplied by the architect or millwork (joinery) company, it is necessary to visualize the piece. You may want to re-draw supplied drawings, make tracings, research similar designs in resource books or create a three dimensional clay model in order to understand fully the function and the appearance of the carving to be done. If the blanks are supplied by a joinery company, check them for accuracy against the drawings.

Ensure the bench and tools are in good working order. This should go without saying; stopping in the early stages to sharpen tools, find the mallet or sweep the floor doesn't allow momentum to gather or, in carving moulding, a rhythm to develop.

Sequence

Decide on the sequence of the work. Familiarity with the design as explained above helps in figuring the order of operations in fabricating the material to be decorated. Many decisions depend on one's available equipment (that is, gouges) and millwork or cabinet making experience. Usually the success of one operation depends upon the preceding task, and often there are several ways to do the same procedure. One example is making the blank for a keystone. Most keystones have sloped sides and many have sloped front faces so there is a dilemma as to which of the two to machine first.

It is vital to determine a sequence of gouges to be used to achieve the desired effect. The picture shows egg and dart moulding partially completed compared with a completed section. Practice the sequence on an extra blank so that each step is logically thought out. When satisfied with the outcome, remove all extraneous tools from the bench. This is particularly applicable in a repetitive activity such as runs of moulding, but this is not so easily done when you are carving a complex relief like a floral garland. With possibly several dozen tools on the bench one must develop a system to find the required one without

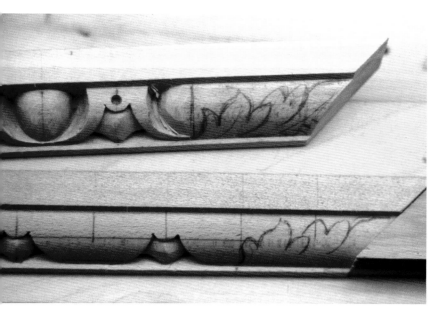

Left **Egg and dart moulding completed, compared to a partially completed section**

Above **A variety of tool handle shapes**

wasting time. As is often suggested, tools with different shaped handles or with some system of colour coding may prove to be helpful. The picture above shows a variety of tool handle shapes. Another time-honoured method is to arrange your gouges on the bench, placing shallow sweep gouges on the right, the middle sweeps in front and the deep sweeps on your left. What seems to happen with me is that I use a basic group of three or four gouges for much of the work and occasionally rely on others, thus a hierarchy of gouges develops.

Right **An overall view of the fence side of the work station with moulding held against the front fence**

Securing the work

The first rule of safe carving is to secure the workpiece. This is easy for most projects by using bench dogs, clamping the work to the bench top or, less commonly, holding the work in a vice. The work station such as described in my book *Carving Classical Styles in Wood* is a versatile holding apparatus. The work station is a piece of ¾ inch (19mm) thick plywood outfitted on one side with fences. A number of additional fences, spacers, cams or wedges allow a variety of shapes to be held with a minimum of jig-making. The picture above is an overall view of the fence side with moulding held against a front fence. Pictured above right is a detail of a pierced carving being held by a floating fence and tightened with cams. Pictured right is the reverse side of the work station (carving screwed from underneath) and tools arranged in an orderly fashion, some in a tray. I have accumulated a number of specialized, shop-made holding devices.

I have several lengths of stock approximately 3 x 2 inches (75 x 50mm) with V-grooves in them to hold mouldings at a comfortable angle. I also have several lengths with shallow dadoes just wide enough to jam specific moulding widths into them, and many scrap pieces of plywood with routed recesses which, in conjunction with double sided tape, hold small blanks. The picture on page 20 shows the use of a special recess for holding small carvings.

I also have several pieces of plywood with a grid of countersunk holes to accommodate screws so that multiple blanks can be held

Right **Details of a pierced carving held by a floating fence, tightened with cams**

Below right **The reverse side of the work station (carving screwed from underneath) and tools arranged in an orderly fashion**

simultaneously. I have fences with cleats, pillow blocks and negative profiles to clamp various mouldings, and even some tapers to hold finials with drilled holes while carving them on the lathe. But some custom jigs which are specific to one size or shape blank are discarded upon completion of the commission because I rarely carve the exact same element again.

My hierarchy of holding preferences (of a flat-backed panel), reflecting what I perceive as efficient, might be something like this: between bench dogs, C-clamped to bench top, screwing into back of blank through plywood (or work station) and lastly, the newspaper/glue method. Of course, sometimes the blank can be fabricated with extra material like tabs so that it can be held safely with C-clamps. For example, in order

to hold a number of small circular blanks of carved rosettes, cut stock thick enough to accommodate the rosette and provide a base to be clamped or held by bench dogs. See the drawing below. Remove the drill bit and use the desired hole saw in a drill press to define the circular blank.

Cut three-quarters or so into the material and space the circles along the stock. Use a dado blade or bench chisel to clear out the waste between the circles, leaving raised cylinders for carving the rosette. After carving, use a backsaw to free the rosette from the stock.

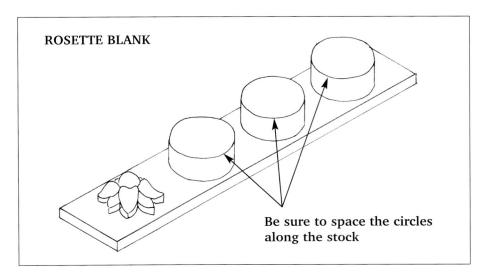

ROSETTE BLANK

Be sure to space the circles along the stock

Above **This shows the use of a routed recess for holding small blanks**

Left **Drawing of rosette blank. Blank for carving multiple small rosettes**

Technique

Technique is a tough subject to tackle in a short explanation as it involves many subtle things. Technique may be determined by species and quality of wood, but primarily encompasses the sequence and appearance of cuts. Bench planes cut with one sweeping motion so the (flat) surface 'reads' well. A broad carved surface, on the other hand, often has many facets created by repeated passes of the gouge. Of course, there are occasions where texture can be enhanced by parallel tool marks. Crisp edges, the degree of undercutting and boldness of relief are also factors determined by technique. Compare the pictures right and below, noting respectively the flowing oak leaves, geometric precision and delicately pierced

Above **Flowing oak leaves**

Below left **Geometric precision**

Below right **Delicately pierced foliage**

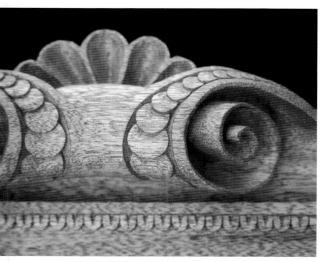

Right **A round nosed chisel can be used to carve the interior angles of the coves associated with Gothic tracery**

foliage of the appliqué. If you are carving multiples, the same operation should be done on each piece before proceeding to the next step in the process. Securing all pieces side by side or spaced along the bench is the most efficient way to achieve this. If you do one operation all the way through the set of blanks, correcting errors is easier because visual comparison is easier.

To be truly efficient, you must learn to carve with either hand (reversing direction of cut by reversing hands). Not only does this preclude wasting time by the frequent need to unclamp, re-position, and re-clamp, but having to think about what you are doing with the less proficient hand promotes visualization. Most people with effort and mindfulness can achieve some degree of ambidexterity.

Dedicated tools

Don't hesitate to modify tools to create 'dedicated' equipment for specific cuts. As an illustration, I will mention one I use frequently. I carve a lot of Gothic tracery and the round nosed chisel is the perfect tool for cleanly carving the interior angles of the coves associated with the style as shown above. Different widths are needed for various sizes of coves so I purchased a set of bench chisels and reground them to have a semicircular leading edge bevelled around the curve.

Many carvers have their own suggestions, from extremely front bent tools to skewed fishtails to gouges with forward or backwardly ground wings. The purpose of modifying tools is to make a certain cut cleanly and easily; sanding take lots of time and in many instances is aesthetically undesirable.

Right **Modify your tools to suit a special situation**

Below right **The shop-made sliding marking gauge**

You can also make specialized layout or marking aids. The one I use most often is a cabinet-maker's marking gauge outfitted with a pencil, but I have also made a similar gauge for marking inside a border (in a recess) or over an obstruction. It consists of a 'fence' of stock about four inches (100mm) long with a sliding bar and, again, outfitted with a pencil which can be adjusted up and down.

Pointing machines as illustrated below right are easily made from scrap and dowels to check depths or transfer measurements from a model to the carving. The picture also shows a thin board with a pencil through it used as a depth gauge. Sheet metal or rubber can be used as a straight edge bent around curves (as on moulding profiles). A well made brass hinge can be used to continue a mark around an edge. Of course, the sheet metal pattern for multiple layouts as on mouldings is a well-known trick of the trade.

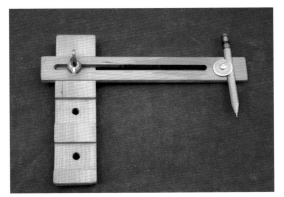

Concentration

Quality work comes from concentration and confidence. Though it may sound crass, one has to limit one's interruptions by letting the answering machine intercept calls, or having certain 'office' hours or limiting walk-in traffic.

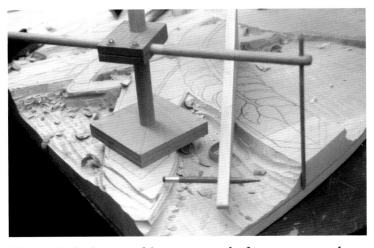

Above **Pointing machines are made from scrap and dowels. The board with pencil is used as a depth gauge**

Above **A garland**

Only experience (practice) can provide confidence, but technique which is well thought out, as outlined above, and eschewing fussy cuts and inappropriate detail helps. Many novices think that detail denotes an impressive carving and spend hours nit-picking, texturizing and undercutting, but the intention of woodcarving should be clarity of image. Detail should contribute to the viability of the visual 'message'. The most impressive carving follows the principles of design, being unified, having a balanced distribution, displaying an underlying logic and being in proper proportion. In short, a moderately sophisticated viewer should easily perceive the forms of the woodcarving. With confidence you can approach work in a logical, disciplined manner – I needed to conjure up some confidence in carving the highly sculptural garland shown here in detail (picture above).

Confidence

The information supplied in this book will allow you to produce some interesting accoutrements for the home, and should give you the skills and confidence to take on all but the most complex carving projects. The wider range of application of the designs and techniques would include architectural elements, model making and larger pieces of furniture.

Avoiding fatigue

Productivity does not necessarily equate with long hours at the bench. There is an efficiency curve, and it is well-known that everyone becomes tired or distracted over time. Becoming less effective and working while fatigued is not safe. Mistakes in the work also tend to happen more easily and more frequently when you are tired.

To prevent fatigue:

1 Plan to carve while fresh and do other tasks which are less crucial such as sweeping, paperwork, or phone calls when the day is about over.

2 Make sure your bench height or other holding situations are comfortable ones. If you generally stand at a bench to carve make sure the floor has a mat of some kind to reduce leg and back strain. If you sit while carving, have a comfortable chair.

3 Keep tools sharp; dull tools lead to frustration (tension) and require more physical effort.

4 You may want to wear gloves while carving, especially while roughing out with a mallet. Anti-vibration, padded gloves without fingers are available from woodworking supply houses. Make sure your joints do not become sore – some operations, such as holding a gouge by the shank to place it accurately, can fatigue fingers. Taping a dowel or half dowel or similar piece of the wood to the blade will help by providing more to hold.

5 The ability to sustain concentration varies with each individual, but it is a good idea to step back and eye the work from time to time. Do some light stretches to prevent muscle fatigue and cramped fingers and take short disciplined breaks.

6 Learn to change hands, carving from the left as well as the right distributes the effort.

Practice is the best way to become efficient. For the creative mind the apparent boredom of repetitive carving is an anathema, but to the trade carver the challenge is in finding efficiencies and developing rhythms, making behind the scenes ornament seamless with the overall building of a piece of furniture.

I do not promote haste in carving and hope that these comments will, in fact, slow you down. Efficiency should never imply rushing around in a frenzy, but instead the logical disposition of action. It does imply questions such as, how can I make the process simpler, more direct or easier? Sometimes a few quiet moments save a number of hours.

"Technique may be defined as the method by which an artist finds expression for his art. The technique of his work is good or bad according to the degree in which he has gained control of his material."

Louis McLaughlin, *China Painting*

Chapter Two

The Four Aspects of Craft

◆ **Design** ◆ **Material** ◆ **Tools** ◆ **Technique**

For a successful carving you have to consider the four aspects of craft, introduced in Chapter One, as an integrated process. For the sake of clarity, however, the following discussions take each aspect in turn. I would hope that these comments add to the generally available 'basics' of woodcarving, by concise observation and information gleaned from many years of experience.

Design

Most decorative woodcarving of household accessory items is in a low relief technique and consequently relies heavily on the logic, pleasure and clarity of outline for its effectiveness. That is, the decoration is more two-dimensional or graphic than three dimensional or sculptural. Woodcarving actually begins with a pencil and paper because design is the foundation for an effective woodcarving. Poor design can rarely be remedied by technique and poor technique can fail a good design. Many of the designs in this book began as doodles, as combinations of ideas gleaned from a variety of sources, as sequences of tweaks and failures before being committed to wood. There are lots of exceptions to this two-dimensional idea as sculptural qualities may be part of a larger decorative scheme as shown in the picture on page 136 where the panel in the door is in high relief.

Subject matter and sources

It may seem obvious that you have to decide what you will carve, but I have frequently been asked how I find 'patterns'. You don't have to be an artist to produce effective designs because there are many readily available sources from which to adapt carveable designs. There are books, both new and reprinted, contemporary magazines, furniture and decorative arts collections in museums and historic houses, as well as public buildings. Dover Publications, Inc., Algrove Publishing Limited, and some other publishing companies reprint older carving manuals and pictorial compendiums with literally thousands of designs illustrated. Consult the bibliography for a partial list. There are a few dozen consumer magazines whose intent is to show period and contemporary homes. Don't overlook animal and plant identification books or children's illustrated books. There are many museums around the country which have period or decorated furniture, decorative arts and even whole rooms on display, encompassing architectural elements as well as furniture and accessories.

Walk through most cities and you will see a variety of architectural styles and the decoration associated with them: from classical Greek and Roman government buildings to Victorian interpretations of the Romanesque, from Gothic churches to Art Deco office buildings.

A word of caution is due, however, regarding copyright. Some sources are in the public domain, or unrestricted, but others, such as product catalogues and museum collections are securely guarded. Generally, if you are reproducing an item for your own use (and don't flaunt the work in shows or via photographs) there probably is not an infringement problem. Check with the owner of the item if there is any question. On the other hand, you cannot duplicate a copyrighted item if you intend to sell it. (Emulating your favourite carver's work is flattering and for personal use or limited audiences is okay. It is prudent and morally responsible to give credit to the original carver or designer.)

These sources are good for ideas, for combining different motifs, and for learning the history of ornament. You should keep a file of designs you like for whatever reason, clipped from magazines, from commodity packaging or even old picture calendars. You should have a sketch pad handy for visual doodling, drawing leaves, flowers, honeybees, etc.

Even while adapting from a primary source, there are some 'design principles' or a framework which will help in creating a successful woodcarving. For more detail refer to my previous books, especially *Carving Classical Styles in Wood*.

Composition

Design involves subject matter, composition and treatment. After you have decided the things to be represented (and subsequently) carved, you have to decide the way in which the subject will be arranged in the space. Composition, it can be argued, is the most important aspect of design. A successful composition should have an underlying logic

Left **Look out for pattern ideas everywhere you go**

Right **A successful composition should have a pleasing distribution of elements**

or order, a pleasing distribution of elements, a balance of repetition and variation and a unity of elements. Taking into consideration how the design is to be executed in the material, whether wood or some other medium, is important as well.

An orderly composition allows the viewer to accept as legitimate the subject portrayed. Though some aspects of the depiction may be implied or even distorted, there should be enough connection with general experience to convey the reality of what is intended. Distribution is the placement, spacing and relationship of elements. In all likelihood you will decide the utility of an accessory, such as a bookrack or a candlestick and then plan the decoration which will determine the surfaces which can be decorated. The design will usually have to be included within the construction. Repetition of elements lends a visual 'track record' or reinforcement of the visual cues.

The rhythm of an undulating vine is a common example. The more repetition of an element such as carved mouldings, of course, the more monotonous and, therefore, the less appeal it has as compared with isolated elements which seem to command attention. Variation is needed for balance and to give the design some life. In the end your design should have a unity or harmony of the various parts; too much doubt as to what is represented weakens the enjoyment of the design. Personally, I tend to like a balance between carved detail and plain surface.

Right and Below
It's always worth taking a notepad to jot down design ideas when you see them

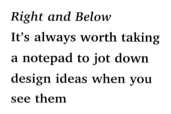

Flamboyant and exaggerated elements piled one on another just don't interest me as much as more contained, or disciplined (classical) ornament. Also, I wonder what the value is of replicating nature with photographic realism. Don't get me wrong, I immensely admire the patience and skill needed to accomplish this sort of objective, but I prefer a more interpretive approach.

Design process

The design process is a series of questions and decisions.

1 What are the areas which can be decorated? Can the intended decoration logically be carved in these areas? Most accessories described in this book and most furniture have borders either for construction or aesthetic reasons. Elements which overlap a border are on the 'inside of the room', bursting out of the restraints of the frame. Breaking the rectilinear parameters creates a more dynamic feeling. The acanthus leaf in the picture right overlaps the border in several places, giving it more life. An uninterrupted border, on the other hand, creates a window which contains and disciplines the carved subject. The geometry of the lid of the jewellery box seems to require a formal (symmetrical) design of oak and laurel branches. A partially hidden element may lend some mystery to the depiction but make sure the viewer can infer the intention.

Above **Copy of the hinged Cincinnati wall pocket. Notice how the design of leaves breaking the frame creates a sense of dynamism**

Above **Jewellery box after Hasluck (see p172). Here the uninterrupted border serves to contain the carving**

2 How will the subject(s) be treated? Will the design and subsequent technique attempt to copy the natural reality of the subject matter or will it be simplified, stylized or even abstracted?

3 Is it wise to assume the viewer will be interested in the subject matter? There are several devices to entice the viewer into the carving. It is more interesting to have an odd number of elements. A flower which has three, five or seven petals is more interesting than one with four or six. Wavy lines are much more evocative than straight ones. Some of the alternation mentioned above includes the variety in individual elements such as the randomness of leaves along a branch. Overlapping elements lend depth, a variety of angles may nudge the viewer to alter his or her viewing angle.

4 Another decision is scale. Size is a gross measurement, but scale involves context and proportion. When all elements seem to have compatibility, and are 'believable', every element is depicted on the same scale. We say they are in proportion. Different sizes of the same thing can be used to show scale perspective; i.e. in a specific depiction of a tree branch smaller leaves in the background can indicate distance and therefore a rudimentary perspective. If a figure has a head as big as its body it is a caricature.

5 Can the design be carved in wood? Wood is a versatile material and most species are relatively strong in thin dimensions. It is difficult to replicate the thickness of a leaf or a butterfly wing. There are techniques to give the illusion of thinness. Review your idea to determine if the material will support the design.

6 What will be the techniques used? The depth of relief will determine how much dependence there is on outline or how much modelling can be done. There is always the question of how the piece is perceived: too much minute surface detailing or intricate undercutting which creates too many shadows may not be the best artistic representation. On the other hand, surfaces which are too broad or not differentiated enough may fail to capture and hold the interest of the eye. Generally, the higher the relief the more ability it has to represent the realism of the natural world. You should also be considering the practical accomplishment of the design by deciding which tools and techniques will be used. The type of relief may depend on location or use of the item. You may have to decide these questions by the tools which are available. For instance, designing a lot of small leaflets on mezzo-relievo acanthus leaves is impractical if you have tools which are too large. On the other hand, you may want to carve the acanthus leaves in basso-relievo by using a veiner to outline them.

Putting ideas on paper

The working drawings which you produce for the project do not have to be overly sophisticated. Usually I start with a mechanical drawing to define the space in which the carving is placed (even if elements of the design overlap a border area). A straight edge, whether a rigid steel ruler or simply a jointed lath, can be clamped to a manageable piece of plywood and used in tandem with a plastic drafting triangle. But much of what you will do is freehand sketching. I often place a piece of tracing paper over the mechanical drawing and transfer sketches I have made on scrap paper to it. I shift the sketches so they fit the area available or to add variety.

Some of the most effective woodcarved decoration is that which complements the object in understated ways and doesn't call attention to itself. All decoration should look as though it belongs, and not 'pasted' on as an afterthought.

Below **Using a drafting triangle while preparing a design**

Material

As woodcarvers, we are concerned with the carveability of our material; ideally the cellular structure or, more generically, the grain, should be straight, even, modestly hard and without defects. Beautiful as wood is in its own right, this is not the primary characteristic desired, because this beauty of grain interferes with the perception of form. Therefore, you should avoid wood having a strong grain pattern. A superb example is the limewood carvings of Grinling Gibbons and the German Renaissance woodcarvers. The dramatic carvings are made from a very unremarkable looking wood.

We are concerned with wood structure and its orientation in the prepared stock. There are a number of books which seek to explore this subject. The classic book is *Understanding Wood: A Craftsman's Guide to Wood Technology*. Several other books deal with specific aspects. For seasoning large billets of wood see *Wood for Wood-carvers and Craftsmen*. James Krenov, in *The Fine Art of Cabinetmaking*, devotes many pages to grain matching and the visual use of grain in creating furniture. Chapters in *The Manual of Traditional Wood Carving* and Dick Onians' book, *Essential Woodcarving Techniques,* also address these topics. There are many factors which influence these characteristics, such as geographical locale, available nutrients, amount of rainfall and so forth. Not to be precious about the notion, but each tree has

Above **Each tree has a history which determines its working properties.**

a history which determines its working properties. One current theory to explain the unusual quality of violins made by Antonio Stradivarius is that the Alpine Spruce he used had dense growth rings because of the cooler temperatures of the Little Ice Age which covered Europe from the mid-1400s through the mid-1800s. This story can be extended to the harvesting and the preparation of the tree for its myriad uses.

We are concerned with the practical aspect of shaping the material and that primarily means understanding the material. 'Reading' the grain is as much a part of woodcarving as knowing the business of each gouge, and though there is much information on the subject, experience is the best teacher. Most species of wood can be carved and the ability to tackle a non-commercial species is one among many reasons why custom carvers are commissioned. But having said that, most carvers have preferences (or price accordingly!): these could be based on availability of species, stylistic or historical fidelity or its working properties.

Left to right **English oak, American white oak, American mahogony and European walnut**

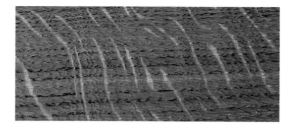 

1 Though you can purchase dozens of species of wood from around the world, many are expensive or endangered, or in a larger sense the harvesting of which is contributing to the global demise. Usually you can find indigenous woods with congenial carving properties. There are several wood finder websites which aid in locating these woods close to home. Some carvers who specialize in one genre of carving usually restrict themselves to the most suitable wood for their chosen technique. Depending on your confidence, you can take one of two approaches: to carve a variety of woods to understand the possibilities and come to your own list of preferences or you can chose a wood considered congenial to workability and rule out cantankerous material as a potential frustration while you learn other aspects of the art.

2 There may be stylistic or historical considerations in choosing a particular species. Historically, the availability of certain species led to their widespread use and to their association with particular styles. Medieval English woodwork is predominantly of English oak (*Quercus robur*) so Gothic styled ecclesiastical furniture made today is (in America) usually of white oak (*Quercus alba*).

Another clear example is the eighteenth century use of mahogany. In reproducing a piecust tabletop you would probably not use course grained red oak (*Quercus rubra*). For an Italian cassone of the late Renaissance use European walnut (*Juglans regia*) or a close substitute.

3 There are physical and visual aspects to grain. From a woodcarver's point of view the main concerns are ease of workability and the clarity of forms. Workability is dependent on several factors: the wood's characteristics as well as the sharpness and use of the tools. You will soon discover that certain woods are better suited to specific techniques than others. For instance, incised carving or outlining a design with a parting tool is best done on a relatively soft and even grained wood, such as basswood or mahogany. Some woods require more use of the mallet, especially for bosting. Harder and tougher woods require a more obtuse cutting angle on your gouges and a substantial back bevel in order to strengthen the cutting edge.

Carving properties

Because I do a large variety of commission work I don't have one favourite wood. I also understand the appropriateness of various woods for particular historical styles or for

specific uses. To me it seems that air-dried wood has better carving properties than kiln dried wood which tends to be harder and more brittle. I very much like the workability of air-dried American black walnut (*Juglans nigra*). Not only does it have marvellous carving properties, but it has a much richer colour (than the 'muddy' homogenization of steamed cured material) and some character which some woods, like basswood (*Tilia americana*), don't have. I also think that white oak is easily carved when air-dried. American basswood is recognized as a congenial wood for the amateur as it is quite soft and has bland grain. Using such a wood allows the novice to concentrate on technique and not on the proclivities of the wood, so consequently it is used in many woodcarving classes. European lime, though often equated with American basswood, is somewhat harder and firmer. I don't recommend using basswood for any of the projects in this book, however, because it is liable to be damaged by everyday activity. In most of the projects any of the following woods could be used: walnut, cherry, soft red maple, mahogany. Of course, there are many others, but these woods are all fine grained, and are relatively hard so they will take detail well, are readily available, and reasonably priced.

A note about mahogany (*Swietenia macrophylla*). It continues to be the queen of woodworking because of its versatility, its character, colour, and working properties, but there are now a number of lookalike woods on the market. Generically called mahoganies, these species may have a similar appearance, but variable working properties, so if possible you should inspect the wood before purchase. Some pieces may display rippled, ribbon or interlocked grain with alternating (or undulating) grain direction which should be avoided.

It is wonderful to have a wide enough piece of wood to avoid the effort of gluing up the required width, but much of the time we are not so lucky. Other than the extra time it takes to glue up a width, there is always a chance that the differences among grain patterns will present a marked difference in colour or grain orientation. It's a good idea to limit the number of glue lines as much as possible. There are several ways to minimize these potential distractions. Planning for the glue lines to be where there are steps or breaks in the design will help to disguise the differences. Also, when gluing up thicknesses, the glue joints should be symmetrically laid out with the middle joint falling on the centreline of the design. The glue lines can act as indelible symmetrical layout lines.

Colouring wood

There is often discussion among carvers about whether or not the carving should be coloured, with one camp decrying its use in obscuring the grain of the wood, the other citing the long history of painted sculpture and the present desire for an absolutely realistic portrayal. You will notice that there is no applied colour, though some stains, on the accessories described in this book. There are many instances in which I would be adamantly opposed to applying paint, but I do not disparage the use of colour, however, having carved and painted dozens of signs and having painted and goldleafed numerous pieces of ecclesiastical furniture and accoutrements. I think it is generally agreed these days that a heavy coating of a glossy finish is detrimental to the enjoyment of an uncoloured carving.

The application of colour should not be a substitute for good carving technique. One exception might be that in some architectonic work (such as the shades of large pipe organs) faux shading might be added to emphasize the depth of carving in a relatively thin board.

The bookends illustrated in Chapter Three show this well – the carved volute sides when glued to the 'core' form the bordering fillets of the top view.

Another way to minimize grain differences is to orient successive lengths of a board the same way. In edge joining boards it is often recommended that plain sawn boards be oppositely oriented to prevent warp, and this may be entirely appropriate to large expanses, such as table tops, but for most accessory items I describe in this book the probability that you would have warp problems is minimal. The possible exception is when a substantial amount of material is removed from one side of the board.

Of the examples in this book, the piecrust tray is the most likely to warp. The best solution to this potential problem is to anticipate it by leaving the blank a little thick. After carving, the back can be planed back to flat.

Grain orientation should be, for the most part, along the longest measurement of the piece. For vertical elements (stiles and turnings) the carved design should reflect this orientation, while horizontal elements (rails and drawer fronts) should be oriented horizontally. There are exceptions to this: delicate areas of the carving may benefit from a certain grain direction, but usually the carved element should conform to the surrounding grain direction.

Right **Gouge, straight shank**

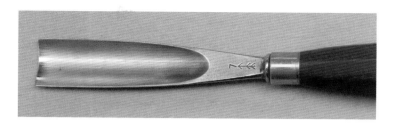

Tools

Almost every woodcarving manual for the past 150 years has addressed the subject of tools and equipment, and little has changed in that time, so I do not want to reiterate commonly available information. Consult the bibliography for some of these instruction books. I hope the following will get you to think about your tools.

Gouges

Gouges are necessary for relief carving because their curved blades (called sweeps) are accurate and efficient in defining (setting-in) and modelling surfaces. Observe any of the low relief projects in this book to realize these carvings would be very hard to accomplish with only the use of a knife.

The most impressive thing about gouges is their abundance and variety. For the intimidated novice the minutia of designation may be thoroughly academic. They may be satisfied with a relative nomenclature of 'shallow', 'medium' and 'deep' curved edge. The carver who is seriously attempting traditional decorative woodcarving, however, knows that each tool has a particular sweep or curve, and consequently a specific use, and it behoves them to appreciate differences in tools such

that they become second nature. To keep track of this variety, manufacturers have devised systems of numbering to differentiate each tool. There are inconsistencies among these systems, but in western tradition, when considering the straight shanked or 'regular' tool, each listing equates lower numbers to shallower sweeps (#2 and #3) and higher numbers to the deeper sweeps (#8 and #9). There are other carving tools which, though worked into the systems, are different from the usual single radius tools of the above spectrum; such as chisels, U-shaped veiners and the V-shaped parting tools.

Other than sweep there are additional considerations, the primary ones being widths and shank configuration. Width is the measurement across the blade from side to side and not the actual length of the arc described by the curving blade. Another aspect of gouges is how the shank, the metal between handle and blade, is shaped. Straight shanked tools retain the axis orientation of the handle, while long bent tools curve from the handle axis so the cutting edge is below the axis. The front bent tool is straight shanked until the last third (or less) where it bends away from the handle axis dramatically. The back bent is

Left **Detail, back bent gouge**

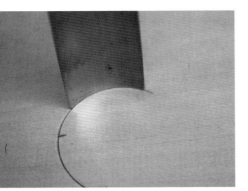

1 A self-tracking circle

2 The degrees of arc

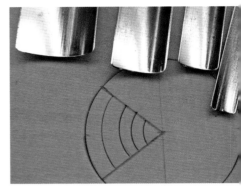

3 A family of gouges cover the same degrees of arc

similarly configured except that where the shank curves the sweep is arching upwards, the opposite of the usual orientation. It must be pointed out that sweeps vary among manufacturers and as depicted in their catalogues, so comparisons are sometimes frustrating. The best way to relate the tool to what it does and its relationship to other tools is to perform a simple exercise. Use a scrap of dressed soft wood (basswood) or a piece of firm cardboard. Hold the tool perpendicular to the surface, press it in enough to leave a curved impression the width of the tool (1). The sweep of a gouge is intended to be an arc of a circle or a segment of a circumference so if you now rotate the tool by sliding it from the original impression it should 'self track' a near perfect circle. If the circle, after a few tries, refuses to appear, you may have a blade which is not symmetrically made. As you will see upon repeating this procedure on various gouges, different widths of the same sweep produce circles with different diameters. Each gouge, therefore, covers or describes a certain number of degrees of a circle. It is important to note that gouges of the same sweep cover the same number of degrees of arc regardless of width. To illustrate this, mark the extent (width) of the tool around its circle (2). Then find the centre of the circle by using a circle template or geometrically with a compass. Draw lines from the centre to the marks defining the arc degrees of the gouge. Now select other width gouges of the same sweep and place them between the angled lines such that they are concentrically oriented (3). This comprises a 'family' of gouges, in the illustration they are #7 sweeps (4).

Why is all this interesting? First, it establishes a family of gouges describing concentric circles, each member covers the same portion of their own circle. Shallower gouges cover a smaller portion of their circle than deeper (more curved) gouges. The #9 gouge is a semicircle, describing 180 degrees. Second, because there are equalities or overlaps among different sweeps and widths. In the picture (5) the narrower #3 gouge and the #5 match exactly the circle described by a wider #7. Third, as the picture shows (6), the same width of different sweeps describes different diameter circles. Knowing this sort of

5 Different gouges describing the same circle

4 A family of #7 gouges

6 Above right **The same width of different sweeps describe different diameter circles**

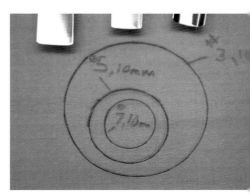

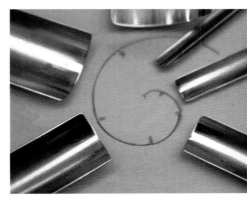

7 A family of gouges describing a spiral

information enables you to set-in spirals using a family of gouges because of the increasing (or diminishing) circles they describe **(7)**. The sample boards in Onians' *Essential Woodcarving Techniques* and Wheeler and Hayward's *Woodcarving* are certainly worthwhile doing to understand your tools.

Buying tools

When purchasing tools you should inspect them carefully. The primary concern is the metal blade and how it is formed, though the quality of the metal is only discernable after use, most of us lacking scientific knowledge or capability to evaluate metals. Logically enough, the smaller tools are asked to do less removal of material than larger tools and therefore require less force to perform their jobs. More metal, however, is not necessarily a good thing as cheap tools often have thicker sections of lower quality steel. This relative thickness to width and sweep ratio is difficult to quantify, but if in

hefting the tool it is heavier or lighter than expected, evaluate carefully.

Hold the tool so that you sight along the shank, observing first the symmetry of the cutting edge curve, the evenness of the section and the alignment of the shank with the handle. Inspect the bolster, or shoulder, as the shank enters the handle to see that it has a flange perpendicular to the shank and abuts the ferrule or handle flatly. See that the bolster, ferrule and wood handle are well fitted and do not have any edges which might tire your hands.

Purchase straight shanked tools first. Don't purchase long bent tools unless you plan to carve a lot of bowls, in my work I rarely use them. Do not buy more than a few front bent and back bent tools. I use several narrow #3 front bent tools for grounding in tight spots. Eventually, you will purchase several back bent tools for rounding vines,

Recommended Tools

1	#3, 20mm
2	#3F 8mm (fishtail)
3	#3FB, 3mm (front bent or spoon)
4	#5, 8mm
5	#5, 20mm
6	#7, 6mm
7	#7, 10mm
8	#7, 14mm
9	#9, 10mm
10	#12, 6mm (parting tool of 60 degree angle)
11	#3, 12mm
12	#5, 5mm
13	#5, 16mm
14	#1, 5mm (skew chisel)
15	#2, 5mm
16	#7, 20mm
17	#9, 6mm
18	#11, 5mm
19	#8, 8mm
20	#15, 3mm (parting tool of 45 degrees)
21	#3F, 25mm (fishtail)
22	#7, 25mm
23	#8, 16mm
24	#9, 16mm
25	#5BB, 6mm (back bent)

branches and other semicircular shapes. Don't be tempted to purchase fluteroni and macaroni tools – I have never used mine. I do use shallow sweep fishtails frequently.

Almost every carver will recommend different tools, their own prejudiced preferences, depending upon their own range of work. The list of tools (left) attempts to provide a guide for general relief work and as a starting list for carving the applications in this book. I must say that there may be additional tools mentioned in the text which aren't in the first ten tools listed here. I have grouped 25 tools in a hierarchal format. Regardless of whether you follow this list in procuring tools, it is wise to begin purchasing mid widths of a spectrum of gouges and work to fill in sweeps and the two extremes of width. Shallower sweeps tend to be more versatile than deep sweeps. (Numbers refer to Pfeil brand 'Swiss Made' tools listing.) This list does not have to be followed pedantically. I did not list alternatives or substitutions. You may even want to modify or create new tools to address specific situations. I often

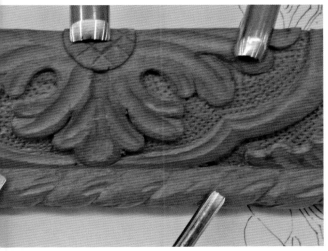

Left Moulding with tools. The tools used to make the design are adjacent to the cuts they produced

Below A favourite gouge, fishtail #3

Above Modified #11

use a fishtail chisel, a round nosed chisel and a #11 with wings ground back. The first is made either from a carver's fishtail chisel which has two equal bevels or from an ordinary bench chisel. On the former, one side of the blade is flattened, making it like a bench chisel, while the sides of the shank of the bench chisel are ground to replicate the fishtail. There are many uses for this tool, including cleaning vertical walls, clearing acute corners and, turned over, as a mini-plane. The second tool is made from a regular bench chisel with the blade ground to a semicircle (or an elliptical 'nosed' or thumbnail silhouette) as explained in Chapter One. The third tool, the veiner, with its wings ground back, making the bottom of the sweep the most forward part of the blade, is specifically used to clean grooves like flutes which abut vertical walls.

I learned to sharpen on oil stones and still do, but I do not disparage the many alternatives, such as waterstones, diamond or ceramic stones, or even micro-abrasive sandpapers. In fact, I have all of these. My process is this: if I have to grind a new bevel, I use a water cooled, slow r.p.m machine, fitted with a gouge holding jig supplied with the machine. I move to a combination stone of aluminum oxide, though I rarely use the course side, but instead the finer side. This is followed with a few passes on a hard black Arkansas stone. I create the back bevel with a round ceramic slip. To de-burr small parting tools I fold micro-abrasives. I then polish with a leather wheel charged with a fine abrasive paste or a cotton fabric wheel charged with jeweller's rouge. A fascinating book is Lee's *The Complete Guide to Sharpening*.

Technique

Technique is more difficult to explain than the other aspects of art because it is less knowledge based, but relies on experience to accumulate its mastery. Technique is the bringing together of the design, the material, and the tools to produce the carving. This is crunch time. Technique is more the *how* than the *why* of woodcarving, the result of the tools actually removing the material to achieve the intended design.

You should be able to look at a design and visualize the tools to be used. To illustrate the relationship of cutting edge to design, study the photograph on pages 40–41. This is a replication of an eighteenth century moulding. The main tools used to create the design are more or less adjacent to the cuts they produced. As you can see, less than a dozen tools were used to produce an attractive and seemingly complex design. It is a shallow though detailed relief carving on an ovolo profiled moulding.

Don't confuse technique with design: the depth of relief of a griffin or the overlap of oak leaves are not considered part of technique. The clarity of cut or the treatment of the surfaces would be included in technique. The following, then, are some general comments on technique, which summarize much of what is explained throughout this book.

Enjoying the process

In our time-sensitive lives we are focused on results and often forget that proficiency comes with practice. Though the custom of a long formal apprenticeship is part of the historical past, you should always approach your work as an apprentice would – observing, learning, experimenting and practicing. Refrain from being overly goal-oriented and enjoy the process for its own sake. Wood is relatively cheap, believe it or not, when compared to the hours invested in a carving. So don't hesitate to carve up a piece of wood, even a 'nice' piece. It should be a large enough piece to have clamps out of the way. One rule which should never be ignored is to *secure the work*. Accidents to hands or the work are likely to happen if the material slides, rocks or tilts. Here are several suggestions. Choose a medium sweep gouge such as a #7 gouge of $\frac{1}{2}$ inch (13mm) width. Cut straight lines across the grain, beginning with just lightly scooping the surface. Now shave a little deeper, but leave a little of the blade on either side above the surface of the wood. This is a good test to determine the sharpness of the tool – any streaking or tear-out will immediately demonstrate a less than optimal edge. There will be some effort in passing the gouge through the wood with a dull edge when compared to the sharp edge you will now make by sharpening the tool. Repeat this exercise with different sweeps, noting the differences in process and result.

Left **An assemblage of carving samples provides a valuable reference for future work**

Watch the tool cut; literally, watch the tool as it cuts the material.

Carving straight lines along the grain, instead of perpendicular to it, is a little difficult as the tool, especially a parting tool, tends to follow the fibres of the wood, producing a wavy line. This difficulty is negligible in soft, even-grained woods such as basswood, but is a larger concern with hard course grained woods such as red oak. It is even more difficult if the grain is rising against the tool, so you should try to carve 'with' the grain. A simple test of trying either way will immediately indicate which is the more genial direction. Yes, you can carve against the grain of many woods.

Now practice making arcs or curves. Plant the heel of the hand gripping the shank of the tool on the material and pivot the tool using your upper body. One side of the tool is cutting against the grain of the wood while the opposite side (or wing) of the gouge is cutting with the grain. You want the tear-out to be on the waste side of your design. It is best, then, and particularly on more problematic woods, to work the circle by quarters, carving across and then with the grain. A spiral might also be practiced in this way. I advocate practicing the intended techniques to be used on your project; whether deep grooves, setting–in small leaflets, or grounding in tight spaces. This is especially helpful to establish the sequence of cuts, the tools to be used and to provide a chance to evaluate the visual effect of the carving. For some designs a formal 'sample' is wise for the sake of record keeping, for a valuable reference for future work, and as a sample to show clients. The sculpture of the picture above is made from samples and practice pieces.

Lighting

Lighting is often mentioned but then forgotten by most carving manuals. Everyone's situation is different, but whether working in a basement, garage, studio or living room one should have strong enough general lighting to see the work clearly. It is helpful to be able to adjust the source of the light, whether by turning off some fixtures, by moving fixtures or by turning off all fixtures and benefiting from the natural light coming in a window. Take your practice piece and rotate it under a strongly slanted light source and note how some lines (edges) seem to disappear. Incised carving and fine surface texturing rely heavily on a directional lighting situation. One test is to take your carving outside on a nice sunny day – you might be surprised at the fuzz in the corners or the surface with the glaring facet at odds with the overall pattern of facets, or a little nick or curved mark of a #5 gouge in the ground.

Consistency

Here are several suggestions for cleaner, crisper technique. First, be consistent in every aspect of the work. This regards setting-in, grounding, modelling, and texturing. Many students, too eager to finish their piece, disregard this sequence and then are frustrated to have to return constantly to clean up or redefine areas. Generally speaking, and for setting-in, use the largest gouge which accomplishes what needs to be done. Consistently use the same tool for the same cut everywhere on the piece or on multiples. There are times when it may be advantageous to use a smaller width of a shallower sweep to continue a long curve, such as when curves intersect making an acute interior corner. Larger gouges have thicker blades and so the bevel prevents much depth in these situations; a thinner sectioned tool is more apt to clean such angles better. You should match the tool to the outline or curvature as much as possible (and your available tools allow), as this avoids a lot of pesky fibres clinging to the interstices of the carving. When in doubt, use a shallower gouge so that the wings don't nick the intended outline. But, in any event, you should clean as you go.

Left **Ensure your work place is in a well lit area**

You should 'ground' a relief to a near finished depth around the entire relief before proceeding to modelling. The ground should be even; a sideways view of the 'walls' readily shows differences in depth. Simple depth gauges can be useful to check large areas of ground. Using a handheld router to hog out material creates a consistent depth. Final dressing of the ground and undercutting are done after the relief is modelled.

In modelling, there is a balance to be struck between the necessary reworking of a surface and being so fussy as to over work the surface. Leaving too many different planes or facets, remember, will reflect light differently and instead of presenting a unified surface will only thwart the readability of the form. Less sometimes is more; it is better to 'undercarve,' creating a simplified form than to confuse by fussy details. Variety should be in the design not in the execution.

Ideally, the surface of any plane would be cut in a single pass of the gouge. This, of course, refers to the finished surface which, indeed, may be created with one pass for a relatively shallow relief. In most cases, more excavation of the forms is required before that final surface is determined, but nonetheless all surfaces should appear to be smooth and continuous. In reality, of course, there is a pattern of small facets covering the entire surface. Note how the light reflects from the surfaces. Texturing such as stippling or punching needs to be consistent and is better suited to large relatively flat areas such as backgrounds. Consistency is especially required in texturing as any aberration will call attention to itself. Areas can also be textured by more or less parallel tool marks either of overlapping and random grooves or more consistent flutes.

In the following chapters these four aspects of craft are illustrated by a number of practical examples. All can be used as examples for your own work. I hope that you will adapt them to your own uses and will create your own design preferences.

Right **Stippling is best suited to large, flat areas such as backgrounds**

"The object of decoration is to give interest and added value to the object decorated; if it fails to do this, it is best to omit it."

Benn Pitman, Art Amateur, December 1888

Chapter Three

Wall Pockets and Bookracks

◆ **Wall pockets** ◆ **Rabbit File Holder** ◆ **Bookracks** ◆ **Bookends**

Just about everyone has seen a wall pocket or document holder outside the doctor's examining room holding medical folders, but these utilitarian fixtures are usually tinted plastic and without any hint of decorative embellishment. Wall pockets in earlier times, however, were often made of wood and copiously decorated with relief carving.

Right **A Turk's-cap lily wall box**

Related to wall pockets are bookracks as both are designed to hold things in an orderly manner and, certainly for our purposes, both lend themselves to several varieties of shallow carving techniques and a myriad of designs. Decorating such useful accessories are perfect projects for an amateur carver because they afford an opportunity to practice a number of carving techniques including incised designs, flat carving, shallow relief, as well as edge treatments and lettering. I experimented with different constructions of the simple forms, looking for the most practical designs; ones requiring the least investment in fabrication time and in materials.

Wall Pockets

Twenty-five years ago I made and carved a magazine box, pictured on page 47, which was great for the purpose, but many times since I have thought that it could use some refinement. It is unimaginatively rectilinear and the only decoration is a very shallow relief of a Turk's-cap lily (*Lilium superbum*). It has an almost Art Nouveau verve to its stem and leaves and overlaps the border, but there is little surface modelling and the forms of the flowers are in cartoonish clarity. Though I have not reproduced this box, I was inspired to explore the genre of wall pockets by an example in the collection of art-carved furniture in the Cincinnati Art Museum.

Below **Nineteenth century wall pocket by Cincinnati amateur carver**

Arts movement

This wall pocket and the furniture on pages 11 and 136 are representative of the extraordinary flowering of amateur woodcarving which occurred in Cincinnati during the last quarter of the nineteenth century. Two immigrant Englishmen were instrumental in teaching hundreds of women and men the art of woodcarving. Henry Fry (1807–1895) and his son were professional woodcarvers who taught classes as an adjunct to their business. Benn Pitman (1822–1910), who was primarily a teacher and writer, taught woodcarving in the local art college. The many accessory items and furniture produced over four decades are divided stylistically between the teachers; the Frys tended to use classical motifs such as the acanthus leaf, while students under the tutelage of Pitman followed his solidly Aesthetic Movement principles and his adamant use of native plants.

The Aesthetic Movement is hard to define because it was a cultural mood or atmosphere with diverse manifestations permeating everything from architecture, fashion, various crafts, book illustration, porcelain painting, play writing and all attributes of self-conscious aesthetic living. The movement began in 1860s Britain with a determination to change what many considered a moribund design vocabulary dependant on foreign ideas and expertise. Peaking in the 1880s, the tenets of the movement continued to influence the decorative arts well into the twentieth century. Stemming from the eighteenth century philosophic musings on beauty and art, the nineteenth century had protracted discussions (via Ruskin, A.N.W. Pugin, Owen Jones and many others) of these issues, spawning a number of craftsmen, artists, writers and architects to address the various aspects of art, craft and the interpretation of beauty. The Aesthetic Movement grew from a new found confidence in British design and from the disgust with overstated and deceptive decoration. There was the notion that elegance and beauty could be embodied in everyday objects; but the dictum of Art for Art's Sake is sadly misguided. The perceived simplicity of Japanese domestic arts was very appealing as was the 'honest' work of the medieval tradesman. Consequently, the design and subject matter echoed these influences, the Pre-Raphaelite painters being a familiar example. The ideas of John Ruskin (1819–1900) greatly influenced the formative years of the movement, 'advance(ing) the argument that the decorative arts, handcrafted and utilizing nature as a design source, could be morally elevating' (*Cincinnati Art – Carved Furniture and Interiors*). William Morris (1834–1896) picked up the proselytizing banner in an effort to improve society by a life is art and art is life sort of philosophy. As a consequence, there was much emphasis on home culture and amateur work.

Cincinnati wall pocket

The Cincinnati wall pocket pictured on page 48 is composed of two boards of black cherry (*Prunus serotina*). The back board which is mounted on the wall has a silhouette found in other pieces made under the direction of Benn Pitman. It has a floral carving (possibly oleander (*Nerium oleander*) in a recess of a Gothic arch. The grain is oriented vertically. The front side has a trumpet vine (*Campsis radicans*) motif in a raised panel frame with the grain running horizontally. The pieces are held together by two hinges at the bottom and chains attached with eyehooks on either side. The wall pocket, as one student recalled, was the first student project because it offered many lessons in technique and was of simple construction.

Typical of Pitman's student's work is the use of indigenous vegetation and flowers as decoration. Undoubtedly, live specimens were presented to the classes, but Pitman must have used an illustrated botany identification book as well. Some students probably had taken sketching classes at the art school and most had flowers and plants around their houses. In Cincinnati pieces there is often an unsettling juxtaposition of naturalism and stylization, however. On one hand, stylized flowers seem simply filler (rows of rosettes or diaper patterns, for example), while naturalistic representations look like botanical studies. Rarely are flowers gathered together in a classical sort of 'unnatural' garland or bouquet. Today, nature field guides are good design sources, especially if they have line drawings which can be easily adapted to shallow relief. If you are interested in the symbolic meaning of flowers, as was popular in the Victorian era, Susan Loy's book *Flowers, the Angels' Alphabet* has an extensive listings of flowers and their associated meanings, compiled from many publications of the nineteenth century.

Constructional considerations

Thinking that the hinges and chains of the original Cincinnati example were used for adjustment, making the apparatus collapsible if one ever needed to transport it somewhere, or expandable to accommodate more items, I wondered if magazines (which seemed like the most probable contemporary use) would settle in the acute angle in an orderly manner. In the first version, the rabbit file holder, explained in detail below, I used an angled block between the two flat boards. Screws and glue held the pieces together. Though this construction is illustrated in *The Manual of Traditional Wood Carving*, I was worried that leverage stress might cause the joint to fail. It has not showed any signs of coming apart though it is constantly overloaded with manila folders and, in fact, I subsequently copied *The Manual's* design of the thistle which uses this construction. In a second version (see pictures far right and bottom right) I added connecting sides to satisfy my misgivings.

Left Butternut box with carved wood anemone and oak leaves

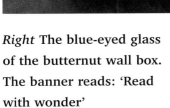

Right The blue-eyed glass of the butternut wall box. The banner reads: 'Read with wonder'

Above Side view of the butternut wall box

I was still concerned about how magazines might 'sit,' so I designed a third pocket, making in effect a box with parallel sides and flat bottom (see picture on the previous page), thus using the same construction as that shown in the picture of the lily box! This seemed to be the best solution to my concerns: strength, durability and ease of use. However, after making these last two versions – five separate pieces, grooves,

Left **The copy of the hinged Cincinnati wall pocket**

Below **Detail of acanthus leaf**

CONSTRUCTION IDEAS

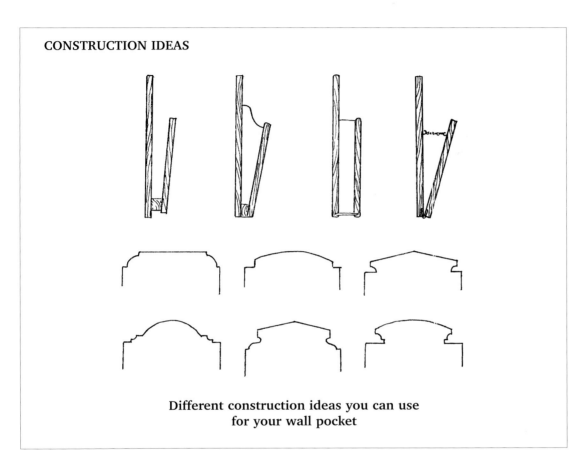

**Different construction ideas you can use
for your wall pocket**

biscuit joinery – I thought again about the uncomplicated nature of the original. I was spending time in fabrication and betraying the 'honesty of construction' tenet of the Aesthetic and Arts and Crafts Movement. Finally, I made a fourth version which followed the original nineteenth century wall pocket in outline as well as construction as shown in the pictures on page 52. The drawing of the different configurations show these examples. In these different versions I also experimented with a variety of woods. I used cherry for the first,

butternut for the second and third, and mahogany for the fourth and for the one with the thistle design.

I realized in working on the second and third pockets that butternut was probably not a good choice because it is soft and tends to be stringy and left some surfaces fuzzy. Some carvers use butternut for figures and non-utilitarian sculptures, but for household items it seems inappropriate. Lighter woods such as maple, birch, white oak, cherry and even mahogany show detail better than darker woods.

The first wall pocket, see below, was designed to hold standard file folders, so the width required glue-up. The front board was cut somewhat shorter to allow the edge carving on the backboard to be seen. The spacer block was initially milled square. This piece was then clamped to the backboard and holes for the screws drilled through the two pieces. The spacer block was then cut with a five degree slope on its front face and set aside until assembly. The backboard was shaped at the corners and all designs laid out. I then routed keyhole slots into the back of the backboard for mounting to the wall; this is much easier to do before assembly. For the design, I thought the rabbit, a symbol for abundant proliferation, was entirely appropriate for an office folder file!

The remainder of the carving explores geometric **edge treatments** and a simple incised **diaper** pattern. Decorative carving along edges as described here is not to be confused with 'tramp art' which utilizes only

Below **The rabbit file holder**

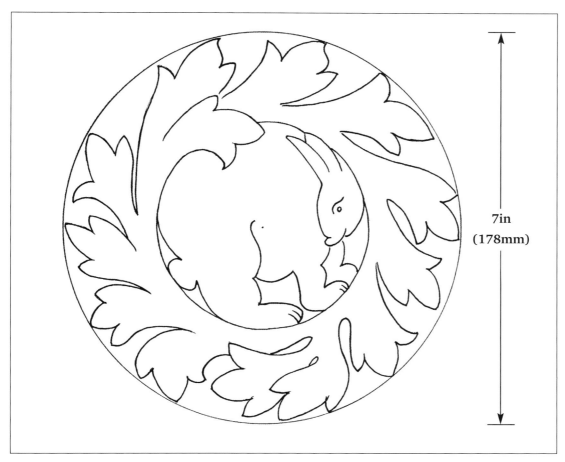

7in
(178mm)

Above **The backboard is 13½ inches (339mm) wide and 14 inches (350mm) tall and the front board is 12 inches (301mm) wide by 10⅜ inches tall (260mm)**

knife-made notches at the **arris** or corner of the boards. The carvers of the latter nineteenth century made use of the technique frequently, and certainly the students of Benn Pitman were taught several varieties.

Similar to mouldings, these designs are composed of repeating units. However, these edge treatments are purely decorative and are carved into the flat surface of a piece of furniture or architectural element (see picture on page 56). Mouldings, on the other hand, are profiled elements, either plain or

embellished with carving, and generally have a practical purpose – they may cover a joint, or visually separate architectural elements, or serve as transitions between them. Edge treatments are usually simple, geometric and have a 'face' side orientation, though some do wrap around the corner. Because edge treatments on furniture are viewed relatively close-up, accuracy is important to make the design unobtrusive; irregularities here would be distracting.

Diapers are usually background 'wallpaper' because they cover flat surfaces and are often 'behind' the main carving. This particular diaper is simply an incised grid of squares oriented at a 45 degree angle to the rectangular space. See also the pictures on pages 115 and 136. A basket weave would work here. A leaf or flower could be used in conjunction with a strapwork (interlaced bands) grid just as well. Try to lay out the grid so that it fills the surface evenly, as a tile layer begins in the middle of the room and works toward the walls. This can be tricky even with rectangles. One thing to keep in mind is that the bottom margin can be adjusted; usually the bottom margin is wider than the top and side margins, anyway. Starting with centre lines, choose an appropriately sized increment by sketching and balancing the accumulative effect with the main carving (here, the circular design). Begin drawing lines which are angled at 45

Above **Samples of edge treatments**

Right **Using the carbon paper method to transfer the design**

degrees from the centre point. If the area were square this line would connect to the corner of the square, but a rectangle is not necessarily so neat. You may have to move side margins slightly as well as the bottom one to make everything work out. Instead of using the carbon paper transfer method, clamp a straight edge to the front board and use a drafting triangle to mark the grid directly, and in this case the two parallel lines (see page 32). The centre rabbit design is then transferred from the drawing by the traditional method of carbon paper and tracing stylus.

Start with the edge carving of the sides of the backboard. After practicing on a scrap piece, lay out the design using guidelines on the face surface and decide on the depth of the ground, marking it on the edge side. For the design here illustrated, set-in the small circular recesses with a #9, $\frac{1}{16}$ inch ($1\frac{1}{2}$mm) gouge at the increment lines. Continue the setting-in with a #7 gouge, the sweep of which produces a pleasant curve.

With a fishtail or a skew chisel approach the triangular areas from the edge and relieve a chip, working to the depth line or ground.

A satisfactory depth for most of these edge treatments is $\frac{1}{8}$ inch (3mm). A round punch (made from a nail) will deepen and make uniform the small circular recesses.

The three semicircles with sunbursts at the top are set-in with appropriately sized gouges and the ground is taken down in similar fashion to the edge treatments just described. The small triangular areas are grounded using a narrow, front bent #3 and skew chisel, and later stippled. The rays are cut to have peaks and valleys. The recessed ground at the top is modelled with a series of flutes. A round-nosed chisel can be used to stop the flutes as they butt against the curving semicircles.

The rectangle of the diaper field and the circle of the rabbit pictorial are defined by incised lines.

Below **Carving the edge treatment**

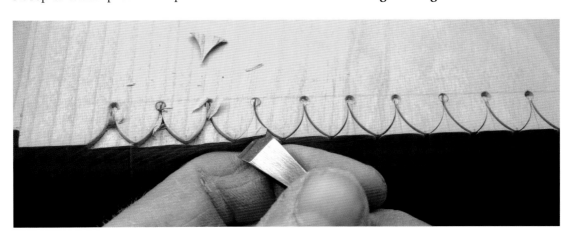

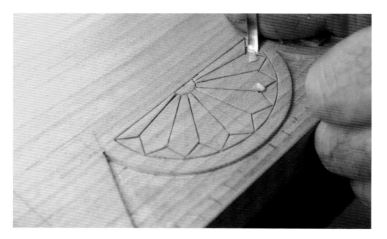

The effectiveness of **incised carving** of this type relies on the line and not on three dimensional form as there is no modelling attempted. (Surface texturing is sometimes used in conjunction with incised carving, but is not modelling in the three dimensional sense). Clarity of outline is, therefore, of paramount concern.

Incised carving is done with a parting tool which is more akin to chisels than

Top left **Using a narrow front bent #3 gouge to ground the sunbursts at the top of the backboard**

Centre **Texturing the ground between the semicircles by parallel flutes**

Bottom left **Using a small round-nosed chisel to clean flute ends**

Below **The incised grid as a diaper**

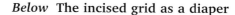

gouges as the 'business' end consists of two straight blades joined to create a vee. Manufacturers make tools of 90, 60, 45, and 30 degrees between the two 'chisels'. Given the same width of tool, the different angles will create different width valleys for the same depth of cut. Conversely, different angled tools will create different depths for the same width of line.

These tools can be deceptively hard to sharpen, but it is essential that they be sharp for this technique. The two wings or straight

Above **An example of incised carving. This tree is revealed by incising through black paint**

sides are sharpened as any bench chisel would be, but there is inevitably a small round at the join which is sharpened with the rotating motion as gouges are sharpened. The necessity is to keep all edges even, avoiding a 'beak' or a dimple at the angle. Though I may at times seem cavalier

Above Another example of incised carving, a line drawing of barn in a landscape

Right A wedding invitation, incised and filled with cream paint. The frame is darkened with asphaltum

about sharpening tools, it is not overly fastidious to count passes on the sharpening stone for each side of the parting tool.

It does help to work material which is moderately hard and close, even grained such as mahogany, walnut, soft maple and cherry. The surface should be smooth before incising as subsequent sanding may obliterate shallow lines. The surface can, in fact, be finished beforehand: the tree in the picture (page 59) is revealed by carving through a layer of flat black paint. The line drawing from a wedding invitation in the picture (left) is incised through a varnished surface and then coloured with cream enamel. The incised vine of the frame is darkened with asphaltum (discussed below).

It is advisable to practice with the parting tool on a scrap piece of the same wood to be used for the project at hand to affirm its sharpness, to understand the working properties of the wood and to judge the quality of line made. The parting tool, especially when cutting diagonally or in a curve, always has one side cutting with the grain while the adjacent side is cutting against it. To ease some of the difficulty thus encountered, start by lightly tracing the line with shallow cuts; subsequent passes will have the tendency to track the original groove. Irregularities or deviations can be corrected, however, by careful sideways emphasis as was done in the details of the barn in a landscape drawing, see the picture left.

Double lines
Returning to the rabbit file holder, the double lines of this diaper grid were made freehand though you could devise a fence for guidance. The squares created at the

Right **The leaves set-in and ground partially complete**

intersections seemed to need an additional element so I placed a small dot with a round punch. The trough just outside the field was made with a #9, ⅛ inch (3mm) gouge, working the depth in several passes.

The foliage of the centre design is set-in and again the ground is recessed using small front-bent tools. The veins are made with a parting tool and the internal lines of the rabbit are parted and slightly relieved. The ground around the foliage is stippled to add texture and visual depth. For more about stippling see Chapter Four. This technique is

Below **A letter pocket of thistle design**

Inset **Detail of the design, showing background stippling**

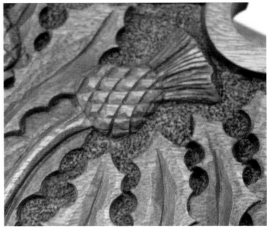

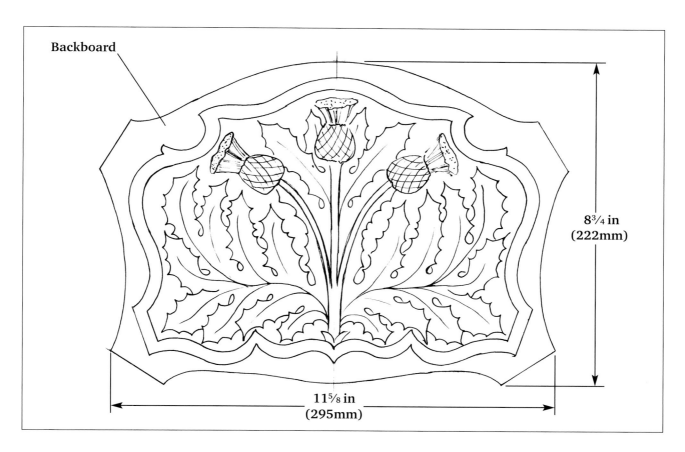

Backboard

8³/₄ in
(222mm)

11⁵/₈ in
(295mm)

Above **Drawing of thistle showing
silhouette of both front and backboards**

often called **flat carving** because the depth
of the ground is minimal, allowing for the
simplest 'over-and-under' modelling. After
final sanding, assemble the three pieces.
The previously drilled holes accommodate
screws, which must be sized to grab the
front board, but not penetrate it. After
dry clamping and starting the screws,
disassemble, and proceed to glue and drive
the screws home.

Stylized thistle

The letter pocket in the pictures on page 62
and the drawing above is made the same
way as the rabbit file holder, but the stylized
thistle is carved in low relief. That is, the
ground is lowered more than in the flat
carving to allow for some modelling. The
thistle design has symmetry, but there is a
little tension between the spiky leaves and
the gentle curves of the silhouette and the
flat band of the border. The depiction is
more realistic than the cartoonish rabbit
because of the increased relief. The
challenge of this design is in grounding the

Left **Wall pocket with acunthus leaves overlapping the border**

small areas between border and the serrated leaf edges. Again, a narrow #3 front bent gouge is required to accomplish this.

On the next two variations (see page 51), I used a router to ground the designs to about ¼ inch (6mm) depth. I carved both versions in low relief, attempting to carve a naturalistic looking bunch of blue-eyed grass (*Sisyrinchium montanum*) on one and several wood anemones (*Anemone quinquefolia*) on the other. To the spindly leaves of grass, I introduced the broader flow of a banner with lettering which balances the linear quality of the grass. To the other, oak branches were appropriately placed above the forest floor habitat of the anemone. I undercut where necessary, but did not belabour the process.

Full Circle

The path of artistic exploration is sometimes cyclical, returning to antecedents and basics. I finally succumbed to the enticing simplicity of the original Cincinnati wall

pocket and decided to make one in that style. See the pictures on pages 48 and here. I used the same overall silhouette at the top and used the raised panel idea for the front piece. Contrary to Pitman's persuasions to depict indigenous plants, I represented the acanthus and the olive. I thought that combining the symbols for Art and Peace were entirely appropriate. I did derive my acanthus design from a panel carved by William Fry, one of the professional Cincinnati carvers. The only complicated aspect of this design was the fact that the acanthus leaves overlaps the border so, after bevelling the border, this 'frame' had to be taken down evenly. This was done efficiently, with a straight bit mounted in a hand-held router.

I had some antique brass hinges and mounted them so that the barrel of the hinge was off-set in order to keep the space between the two boards as narrow as possible. I initially had trouble finding what I thought was the appropriately-sized brass chain, but found a chest lid restraining chain with nice mountings in a hardware supply catalogue. I removed the collar from some small cup hooks for the adjusting end. One obvious drawback to this design is that the chains restrict the size of what might be put in it.

Right **The wallpocket with stained ground**

Finishing

The adage goes something like: finishing makes or breaks a piece. I would argue that the beginning (the design) makes or breaks a piece, but there is no denying that finishing is what is seen first. A poor finish is hard to overcome in order to appreciate an otherwise well designed and carved piece. Preparation of surface is one secret to a nice finish, and this means to use good lighting to study the surface. Lightly sand areas which should be smooth. I believe the prohibition against sanding commonly encountered in the literature stems from the Arts and Crafts movement's philosophy of honest design and workmanship. The answer is to be moderate with the application of sanding, never using it to correct or shape carved surfaces. Usually 380 grit sandpaper or 0000 steel wool is all that should be required. Unless you are experienced in various finishes, I would keep the process as simple as possible. This means not doing more than necessary to protect the carving. Use a clear wax from woodworking supply houses if that is sufficient. I use a penetrating (Danish) oil because it shows (although sometimes dishearteningly) flaws which can then be cleaned up while the oil is still wet. Five or

so coats will build up a slight sheen. High gloss finishes take on reflective properties of their own and can betray the subtleties of form. Even when protective varnish is needed, dull the 'satin' finish with 0000 steel wool.

I finished the two butternut wall pockets with a mix of stains which produced a pleasant reddish brown. I completed the finishing with several coats of Danish oil.

For the rabbit wall pocket, and especially the Cincinnati inspired one, I wanted to replicate the original finish. The cherry and the mahogany of the copy have a similar reddish colour to the original cherry pocket. The backgrounds of the original carvings appear to be quite a bit darker than the smoother surfaces, emphasizing the purpose of the stippling. This darker colour may have been a consequence of using asphaltum varnish as recommended by Benn Pitman in his writings. These days it is used for shading gold leaf and as a primer for painted tinware. When mixed with satin varnish, applied over a carving and wiped

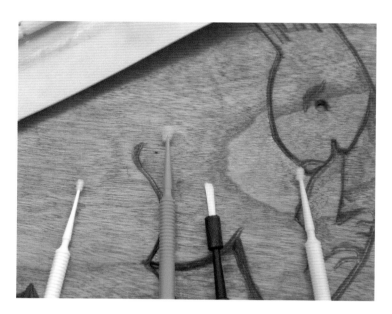

Left **Small brushes
are wonderful for
careful staining**

off, the black colour is retained in the recesses. It does replicate the desired finish, but it seemed a little harsh and is messy to mix and wipe from the carving. The Cincinnati inspired wall pocket uses this mixture as does the vine frame of the picture on page 60 and the thistle letter pocket pictured on page 62. The latter has a more Victorian feel because of its silhouette and the 'ebonized' finish.

For the rabbit file holder, I was looking for something mellow, but not black, with a patina of age. The best way to achieve this effect was to stain the ground with a chocolate-coloured stain and then use a lighter brown for the smooth surfaces. Dark walnut is good for the ground but applying it was ticklish since the stain is thin and runs. It should not be applied to end grain, but only on the surface. I used several different sizes of small brushes, available from artist supply catalogues, though a small round pointed artist paintbrush also works well. Be careful not to have any excess stain clinging to the ferrule of the brush. Slight undercutting is probably a good idea.
I placed the loaded brush in the middle of the area to be stained and worked toward the walls of the carved elements as the stain dissipates from the brush, thus preventing unwanted runs.

After this ground stain was dry, I stained the entire piece with the above-mentioned mix. After drying, I applied penetrating oil over the entire piece and let it dry. On subsequent coats of oil I avoided wetting the dark-stained ground, so that when finally done the surfaces had a nice sheen while the ground was more matt, providing another contrast between ground and carving.

You are probably like me and have a pile of unruly books needing some discipline. In spite of some sci-fi inspired dire predictions, books will be with us for a long time to come and, therefore, we will always need to have bookends, book shelves and portable bookracks. And though there are plastic and metal ones on the market, few have the pleasing decoration which complements the bindings, much less the contents, of the books they hold. You can create a carved bookrack which, by being hand-made, has a story of its own! Without getting into philosophical or historical convolutions; everyday objects decorated in a pleasing way tend to have a positive effect on society as a whole. Don't we admire the painted vases of Ancient Greece (inspiring odes from English poets) or the

Above **A bookrack designed for cook books**

Top **Detail of construction of bookrack**

Above **The second end of the cook bookrack, which shows an empty basket and wine bottle**

colourful kachinas of the Native American Hopi people or the graphic virtuosity of the woodblock prints of Ando Hiroshige?

The construction of these bookracks is fairly straightforward, requiring only basic machinery to dress and cut the mahogany and walnut stock. The joinery can be done by hand, but a router is helpful. Bench chisels are needed to cut the dovetail joints and mortises. Though each rack is made differently, it is the decoration which makes these racks special. The ends are a perfect venue for a wide variety of motif. Because these are functional pieces with a potential for a little wear or damage, incised, flat carving and shallow relief is more appropriate than high relief. And these techniques of carving are perfect for learning the value of simplicity and stylization.

First bookrack

The first rack (see page 67) was designed to hold cookbooks on a kitchen counter and so is decorated on one end with a basket of fruits and vegetables common to Italian cooking. On the other end are carved an empty basket and an empty bottle of wine!

The construction consists of a bottom, two ends and a back brace. The measurements of the pieces are not critical: the length may depend on how many books you have, and the other dimensions on what sizes of book you plan to keep in it. The ends of this example are 9 inches (22.9cm) x 11 inches (27.9cm). Of course, you may design the ends first and cram

Above **Detail of dovetailed end piece and bottom**

in the books as you can! Each end of the bottom is cut with one large dovetail on the table saw. Then the matching recess is made in the vertical side (end) pieces so they fit over the dovetailed ends of the bottom.

A router can be used to waste much of the material. The dovetail recess is cleaned up with a bench chisel. The back brace is made with similar dovetail ends and then let-in to the back of the vertical sides.

This design is a low relief carving of a quarter inch (6mm) using the idea of a wall niche to 'hold' or frame the basket and its contents. Some depth is achieved with some overlap of the olive branch at the side. The basket appears oval, especially in the empty version to further lend some perspective and, therefore, depth. The fruit is rounded to the ground while the olive branch with leaves is slightly undercut. The stones of the niche are defined by barely relieved incised lines. A keystone peeks above the top of the end to break the boring silhouette of the rectangular end.

Left **Bookrack with Art Deco designs**

Below **The opposite end of the picture above**

You can use a handheld router to clear the background of both panels, but the remainder is done with traditional carver's gouges. You can finish this sort of carving with a light stain to even out the colour with a top coat of penetrating oil. A light coating of satin varnish will protect this rack from unavoidable kitchen splatter.

Although this design is a literal representation (reduced in scale), many other styles of ornament can be used to decorate this sort of bookrack; such as specimen flowers, grotesques, greenmen, animals, and so forth.

Second bookrack

Another example of this type of construction which uses an Art Deco motif is shown above. Because the movement, prominent

Curved area 5⅞in (149mm) x 9⅛in (232mm)

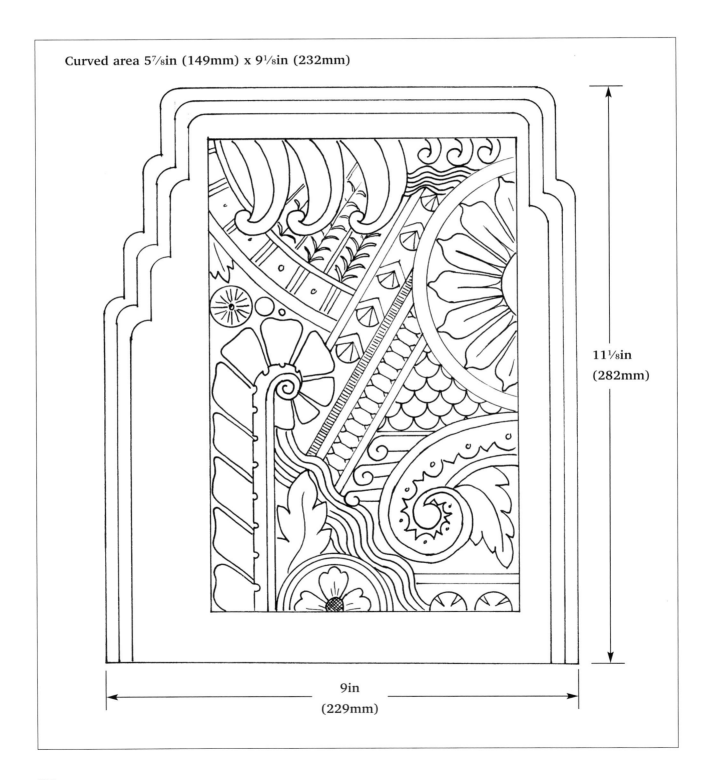

11⅛in
(282mm)

9in
(229mm)

Left **Art Deco design with contrasting straight and curving lines**

Right **Art Deco leatherette scrapbook cover**

between the world wars in Europe and especially in America, celebrated the mechanization and industrial advances of the age, there was little emphasis on woodcarving of a decorative nature in architecture or furniture. In spite of the fascination with geometry, gears and such symbols of mechanization, there are also numerous allusions to classical motifs such as the volute (spiral), scrolling (acanthus) foliage, and even egg and dart moulding.

In this alternative design example, based on a terracotta panel of the period, the surface is divided by groups of elements consisting of straight and curving elements. Though there are several different levels, the various elements can be isolated and worked on separately without much concern for overall integration, or modelling. The apparent randomness provokes the eye to explore the surface, finding intriguing details. A 'stepped' border creates some depth in elegant contrast to the nearly frantic interest of the design it surrounds.

Some of the intrigue of the design is in how it is finished.

The idea was to have the 'chrome' surface of the machine image eroded or worn off to expose the true material of nature, in a sly irony of the Art Deco premise. The wood was first sealed with varnish and then silver paint applied over it. While still wet some of the paint was wiped off, providing a worn or eroded appearance.

Adjustable bookracks

The second group of bookracks are adjustable ones. The example in the picture below has one end secured to a bottom piece using the same dovetail method as previously described while the other end adjusts by placing it in one of three positions. The adjustable end is made with

Below **Adjustable bookrack utilizing mortise and tenon configuration**

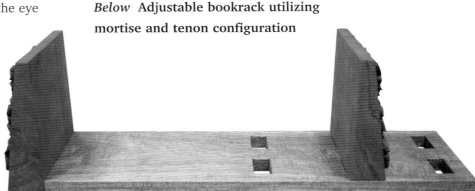

Left **Adjustable oak leaves bookrack**

Below **Detail of oak leaves carving**

Bottom left **Drawing – oak leaves**

7³⁄₄in square (197mm square)

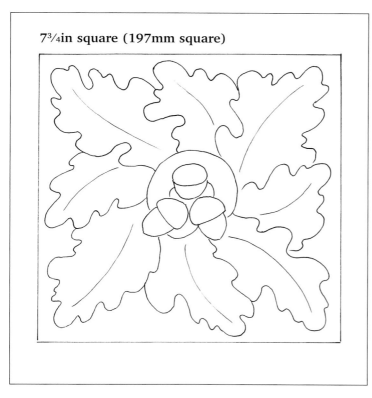

two tenons which fit into sets of mortises in the bottom board. The bottom board should be thick enough to afford sufficient bearing. The thickness of the end also furnishes a bearing surface. To give the illusion of strength (and to show off the carvings!), the two ends slope toward the inside of the rack. The fixed end butts the horizontal base while the adjustable end sits on the base board: this may be a little unsettling (and differing coloured woods don't help), but when placed in the end mortises the slope of the end continues through the slope of the base board. The tenons should fit snuggly into the mortises, but slight play is preferred to tenons which can't be extricated from the base. The tenons are cut slightly shorter than the thickness of the base board, even though you will probably stick cork or felt pads on the bottom to protect the table or desk surface. When the rack is adjusted for the fewer number of books, the extra length with its mortises seems a little awkward. You may want to place your signature or some other subtle decoration here.

Oak leaves bookrack

The design of this example is of oak leaves in moderate relief. Because the ends slope inward there is more material for a higher relief carving and also the chance of accidental abrasion by lamp or other desktop accessory is minimized. The area of the carving is about 8 inches x 8 inches (203 x 203mm). The potential problem with relief of even $\frac{3}{8}$ inches (10mm), as here, is that the orientation of the rack is 90 degrees from the surface (or elevation) of the carving, so the viewer sees the edge of the leaves depicted. Under-cutting may help with something like leaves, but curving them toward the surface allows the

eye to pick up the planes of the leaf from the front of the rack and be drawn around to the side.

One problem with cutting the surface of the end on a slope is that you are always carving end grain. The walnut used here didn't present many frustrating tear-outs, but other woods or grain directions would not be so genial. Flowers would be a good subject for this situation as the stem could spring from the base thickness, and the flower blossom and leaves could occupy the area which would otherwise be sloped away.

Right **The fixed (dove tailed) end**

Far right **The adjustable end showing the continuation of slope on base board**

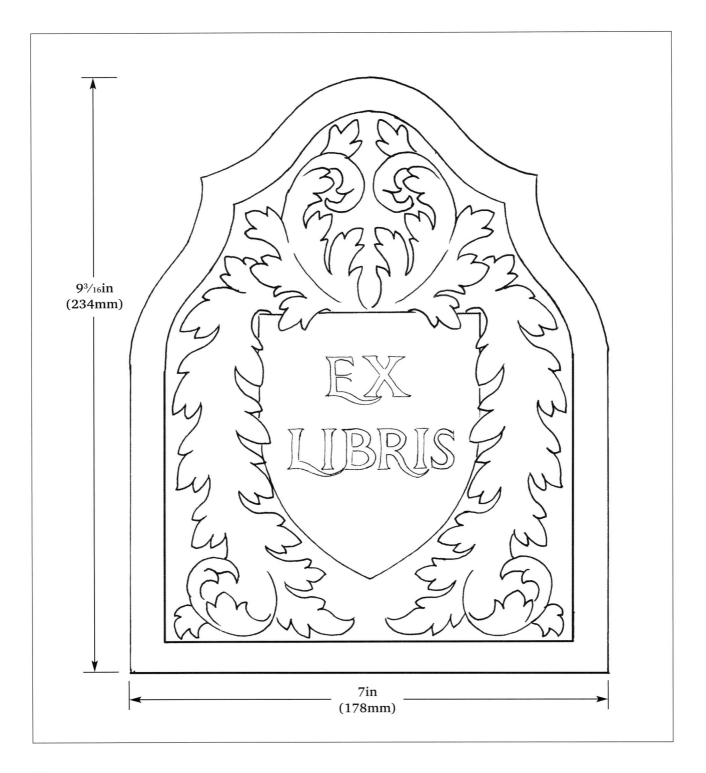

9³⁄₁₆in
(234mm)

7in
(178mm)

Left Another adjustable bookrack, this time with the heraldic *ex libris*

Opposite page A drawing of the *ex libris* bookrack

Below The parts of the base before they are glued together

The two ends of the next example, pictured above, are adjustable along a centre slide integrated into the base board. The ends must have a tab which extends below the surface, see picture above right. These tabs have a hole drilled in them so that a dowel can keep them in place. Ideally, this dowel should be of the same species of wood as the carving. Suitable dowels of some hardwood species, such as walnut and oak, are available from supply houses. Turning a long dowel, ½ inch (13mm) x 24 inches (61cm) is difficult without steadying devices mounted on the lathe. A store-bought dowel stained will probably do just fine. The base is made so that the tabs of the ends fit snuggly between two long sides. It is slightly wider than the movable uprights (7½ inches or

191mm for this example). This is determined by the centre block between the two long sides. This block also holds the dowel which is the keeper of the ends. The ends are carved before the base is assembled. Of course, the base should be clamped dry and the easy movement of the two ends assured.

The silhouettes of the ends have a little more traditional look than the previous examples and the design of a heraldic shield is in keeping with this choice. The depth of relief is only about ⅛ of an inch (3mm), but the overlapping of the shield by the foliage as well as the curling ends of the foliage provide some visual depth. As advocated in some late nineteenth and early twentieth century carving manuals, the ground is eased in with a curved transition between the vertical wall and the flat ground. This gives the impression of the object being carved 'in the solid' and not carved separately and added. This technique would be more apparent and may be more effective on a larger carving, see the waste paper project on page 121. As with many carvings, the time consuming operation of these ends is in the grounding between the small leaves. The blank shield is intended to contain the owner's initials or monogram, or these in combination with the traditional *Ex Libris*. The incised lettering should not be deeper than the ground.

Finishing this rack after assembly is a little ticklish because you don't want the moving parts to stick. Varnish should be avoided. One approach would be to finish the ends first then insert them at glue up. A wax finish would aid in the movement of the ends.

Another type of bookrack is that in which the base expands and the ends are hinged to fold down, making it easily portable.

Above **Lettering detail**

Above **Sliding base and folding ends**

Left **Another portable bookrack**

Example: Bookends

The design of this classically inspired bookend is derived from the architectural bracket found in a number of structural situations – as mantleshelf consoles, as ancones supporting pediments over doors and windows, or as corbels holding up beams or arches. The various carved decorations on these scrolled brackets can be adapted to many other architectural elements – the acanthus leaf and spiral (scroll or volute) being nearly ubiquitous throughout ornamental history. This design is a good illustration of combining the need for geometric accuracy with the more fluid interpretation of natural forms, the essence of architectural carving.

The multi-part construction of these bookends has some definite advantages with only minor drawbacks. Though these may look intimidating to carve, taking the individual elements one at a time is less so. If you don't feel happy with one part, it can be re-done without losing those parts with which you are satisfied. Lack of available thick material might be another reason to use this method. The problem with this method is that assembly is required!

The design of each bookend involves two identical sides and a core, see drawing on page 78. The sides are decorated by a spiral of acanthus leaves sprouting from an 'eye' while the core consists of a geometric profile, a surface treatment and an acanthus leaf. Many renditions of scrolled brackets are simply a long double curve, but the

Above **Classically inspired bookends**

silhouette of these is interrupted by a 'dog-leg' or a short straight line which breaks the flow from convex to concave, making the silhouette more eye-catching.

For ease of construction these bookends are designed to be made in five parts: each has two identical sides, oppositely oriented, a solid middle core and an L-shaped backboard.

I used cherry for its availability, its rich colour, and for its relatively heavy weight.

Make two templates from the drawing: one for the sides and one for the core. The core can be glued up from $1\frac{1}{8}$ inch (28mm) pieces. The sides should be of $\frac{7}{8}$ inch (22mm) thick material. Transfer the design to the side pieces by the carbon paper method or by gluing a photocopy of the design to the blank. (I don't care for this method especially when routing the ground because the edges of the paper fray and obstruct the line). The side pieces are $\frac{1}{16}$

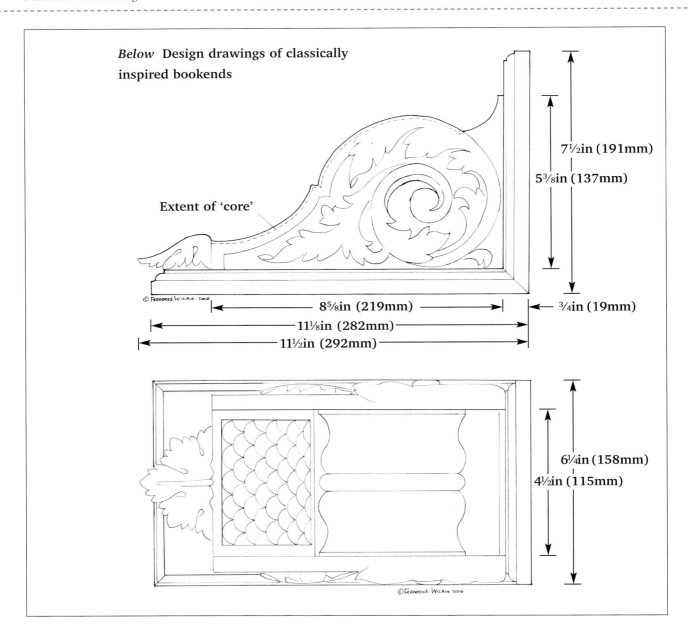

Below Design drawings of classically inspired bookends

Extent of 'core'

7½in (191mm)

5⅜in (137mm)

© FREDERICK WILBUR 2006

8⅝in (219mm)

11⅛in (282mm)

11½in (292mm)

¾in (19mm)

6¼in (158mm)

4½in (115mm)

© FREDERICK WILBUR 2006

inch (1.5mm) larger than the core to better define the border of the core. Dry fit the sides to the core.

The ground of the relief carvings of the sides can be partially routed to a little less than half the thickness of the blank (⅜ inch, 10mm, deep). The two opposite sides can be secured in a work station. Use the appropriate sweeps to set-in the curves of the leaves and spiral of volute. I used the following tools: #7, 20mm, 14mm, 10mm and 6mm; #5, 20mm and 16mm: and #3, 20mm and a #1 carver's chisel, 5mm or #2, 5 mm will aid in clearing interior angles. It is not necessary at this stage to set-in each leaflet, nor clean the ground immaculately. A front bent #3, 4mm will help in excavating deep recesses.

Left Layout of the four sides

Below A dry fit of sides to core

Below left Routed ground

Separate the subordinate leaves by taking them down, especially at their source as they sprout from the main spiral. Begin rounding the smooth outside curve of the the spiral with shearing cuts beginning at the eye. A #5 gouge turned **cannel** down will accomplish this. The eye will be the highest projection with the outer leaves (at the top) the lowest.

Above right Continue the setting-in and grounding process

Right Using a front bent #3 to complete grounding

Left **Begin to set-in and relieve the volute**

Now let's turn to the surface modelling. The leaves should flow from the outside of the long curve of the spiral, and fall back to the ground. The two larger leaves whose tips curl under, are canted slightly with a #5 or #3 so that the curl seems realistic. Model the leaves with long sweeping cuts; the grooves from each leaflet are made using a #7, 6 mm gouge. The cove of the spiral springs from the eye and follows along the spiral. Start by using the same #7 which was used to set-in the eye. Placing one wing of the gouge on the setting-in and the other away from the eye, make a slanted relief cut. This starts the spiral cove. You can continue this stab-and-relieve method a few times, but you will want to switch to a #8, 8mm for most of the cove for a shearing cut.

Set-in the flat border and relieve the ground $1/16$ inch. This ground can be punched to allow the leaves to appear in more relief. (Remember much of the effectiveness of relief carving derives from the contrast of light and shadow and all those little holes produce a darker appearance). Slight undercutting might be necessary here and there to clarify or thin the edges of the leaves.

Middle **Surface modelling; defining the large sweeps of the leaves**

Left **The completed side**

Right **Defining the centre bead of the core with a parting tool**

Below right **Rounding the bead**

The core is laid-out and the centre bead of the convex portion defined by using a V parting tool to separate it from the **cyma** or double curve profile on either side.

An alternative method is to use a chisel to demarcate the valley. Use a #7, 10mm upside down or a back bent #7 to round the centre bead. A larger #7 or #5 will round the convex part of the cyma profile. The larger #7 gouge will rough in the concave part of the profile. Leave a narrow shoulder on each side of the core, thus preventing damage and retaining the edge of the piece. A shallow gouge, #3, is used to fair the transition between the concave and convex. To have smooth surfaces, a modicum of sanding will be necessary.

The scale design is contained in borders or a frame. An **imbrication** is a design consisting of rows of overlapping elements with joints alternating, such as tiles on a roof, scales on a fish, etc. The effectiveness of such a design is in the regularity of execution: this consists of semicircles offset

Above right **The concave section of the cyma curves carved**

Bottom **Two variations of a scale pattern or diaper**

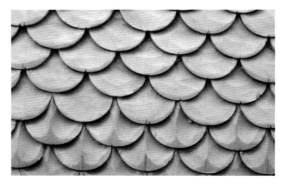

Above **With core secured in vice, carve the scale diaper**

Above **Relieving the scales so that they 'overlap'**

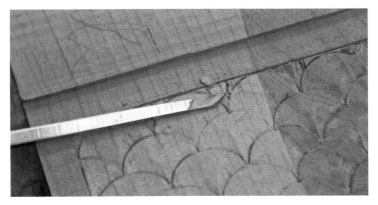

Above **Use a small skew to clean around border**

Right **The completed imbrication**

in alternating rows and relieved so as to imply overlapping scales. A sample should be made with the intended tools in order to work out the actual measurements required; for an even five scales for instance.

The core is best held in a vice and adjusted from time to time for best angle. Because of the nearly end-grain orientation in this situation, you need to be careful in relieving the scales. You should relieve the scales going 'down hill'. In other words, the semicircles are worked from the previous row toward the outer perimeter which is opposite from the usual 'stab-and-relieve' method. This creates a ridge down the middle of the scale. Using the #2, 5mm or a small #3 fishtail, place the corner or wing where two semicircles meet and cut following the curving line. Do the opposite side of the scale. A small skew chisel is helpful in cleaning the acute corners. The picture below shows the completed imbrication.

The core terminates with a typical acanthus leaf. The generic acanthus leaf has leaves which are sub-divided into leaflets. After band sawing the divisions of the leaf, carve the form

Right **The end acanthus leaf slopes toward back, shown in holding cleat**

of the leaf. The flow of the leaf originates in the middle and curves down the centre line in much the same way as the bracket as a whole has a convex and concave profile. The leaf form slopes down on either side at the square end of the scale imbrication.

The head-on view of the picture to the right shows the flow of the leaf. Often the leaves overlap and produce a round or teardrop shaped void between them. (These are also, confusingly, called eyes). In defining the leaflets, it should be noted that as they are set-in the orientation of the tool changes as one works back to the steeper slope of the leaf: from straight up at the middle leaf to an angled attitude at the sides, keeping, of course, perpendicular to the form. Part of this process is to separate the five leaves and to locate the eyes. The centre vein is made by a #12, 6mm parting tool. The #8, 8mm (or 9) is then used for the grooving of the leaflets. Finally, back-cut the leaves with a chisel.

Sand the flats of all pieces, and the geometric profiles of the core piece. Assemble the sides to the core, then mount to the backboard. The L-shaped backboard is mitred and joined with biscuits. Secure the carved piece to the bottom board with several screws and glue. Non-skid cork or rubber pads will aid in keeping your books upright and your reading on the up and up.

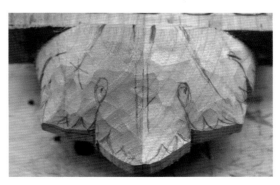

Above **Notice the multi-directional slope**

Above **The eyes separate the three main leaves**

Above **Modelling of leaf**

"Much modern teaching of art rejects the copying of earlier work as a practice likely to stifle self-expression and original creativity...I believe it is fallacy, if not arrogance, to dismiss what our predecessors discovered."

Dick Onians, *Essential Woodcarving Techniques*

Chapter Four

Frames

◆ **Ersatz Art Deco** ◆ **Rustic** ◆ **Florentine**

One of the most common household accessories are picture frames. Frames, of course, can hold mirrors, prints, fabric samplers, photographs as well as oil paintings. There is a lengthy, complex, but fascinating history of framing. Consult the bibliography.

A bewildering variety of frames is available on the market today including ones of metal and plastic, of many colours and finishes, and ones of wood, both plain and fancy. The richly embellished frames of past eras are not particularly in vogue now, being used primarily in restorations and reframing of older works of art. The frames described in this chapter are decorated, but tend to be of the vernacular usage and not the high style or sophisticated constructions associated with the gilded frames of the museum.

Beside their usefulness in protecting art work (or mirrors) and in hanging said pieces for display, frames allow for many varieties of decoration. The frame is linear in nature and often consists of those ornaments which lend themselves to repetition. Some frames are made entirely of classically decorated moulding profiles, scrolling foliage, and diaper patterns. Frames often echo the architectural form and style of ornament in vogue at the time. For instance, the Italian

Renaissance frame had many of the same decorative motifs as seen in frescoes: the grotesque, the scroll, and candelabra, where there are both architectural elements and decorative surface decoration. Meanwhile the baroque frame reflected the exuberance of the undulating surface popular in that style of architecture. Preferred carving woods for frames are walnut, mahogany, cherry and

Above **Frame showing classical elements**

Above **Renaissance frame**

Above **Baroque frame**

oak. Frames to be painted or gilded often are of poplar, basswood or pine, which are also relatively light in weight.

The ornament of many 'carved' frames is actually moulded using composition ('compo') material traditionally made from whiting (finely powdered chalk) and animal skin glue with linseed oil and rosin, according to various recipes. The resulting putty is pressed into moulds. These cast ornaments are then glued in various configurations onto a wood substrate. See the picture on page 85.

Many, though I hasten to add, not all, frames are constructed using 45 degree mitre joints at the corners. This, of course, allows the design elements to continue uninterrupted around the corner. In order to ensure a frame with square corners, you need to cut the joints accurately. A mitre or chop saw is extremely helpful, especially if you plan to make multiple frames. This, of course, can be done on a table saw, or by backsaw in a mitre box.

Small frames can be nailed together, but most require some sort of mechanical joint such as dowels, splines or biscuits. There are several different methods of clamping these joints: the mitre clamp, band clamp, frame or four-way clamp, and various shop made apparatus. The use of a mechanical joint makes clamping and gluing easier.

During the carving of the Art Deco bookrack described in Chapter One, it occurred to me that the design was a conglomerate of disparate elements. I wondered, why couldn't these elements be fabricated from strips of wood, carved with various relatively simple cuts and then glued together to create the sides of a frame?

This design idea was also inspired by a sculptural assemblage I had previously made using samples of moulding and other architectural elements accumulated over the years (see page 43).

Admittedly, this frame will not be compatible with all genres of art, but a style-neutral mirror, or a graphic arts poster, would certainly be complemented by such a frame. It is vaguely reminiscent of the Romanesque usage of various geometric mouldings situated next to each other. I use the same method to produce decorative strips in a utensil box, shown in Chapter Five.

Above **Art Deco frame**

Left **Detail of the frame pictured above**

For the two frames described here, cut long strips of wood to several (three or four) different widths. See the picture on page 89 showing several profiles. Widths of between ¼ inches (6mm) and perhaps ⅝ (16mm), and a wider 1½ inch (38mm) middle piece would work well. Remember that the thickness at the **sight edge** or the inner edge will have to be enough to allow for a rabbet to hold glass, mat, artwork and backing board. An alternative is to have a base or foundation board upon which thinner carved strips are attached. Most woodworking shops produce long cut offs which can be recycled into blanks for this technique.

The best approach for you would be to experiment with different widths, profiles and designs.

What makes this technique attractive is the endless variety of relatively simple design elements and therefore it is a very

Above **Detail of the assemblage**

Below **Practice pieces and 'blanks' in frame configuration**

good opportunity to explore and practice the cuts each tool makes. This example is perfect for learning accuracy of layout, of technique and how light and shadow can be created and used to dramatic effect. Many of the designs or cuts can be made with a common bench chisel, as shown below right.

Other designs make use of various gouges. Many designs can be carved directly onto the flat surface of the wood strip, as in the picture on the bottom of page 90. Strips with profiles increase the variety and depth: with peaks in the middle, or off-set, or with one semicircular profile. Carved strips of the same design can be shifted to create additional variations. You may want to stick in a few more classical details such as the guilloche, rows of rosettes or scrolls. You will no doubt discover many more possibilities than those shown here.

As you explore the possibilities of profiles and develop what might work well, you should have an idea of the size of the frame. The size of the frame might influence what

Above **Sample carvings on various profiles**

you feel is a pleasing overall width of frame and, therefore, the configuration of the constituent parts. If you have pre-determined measurements or standard mat size, you need to begin drawing from the inside of the rabbet, then determine the necessary lip

Below **Possible design made solely with a bench chisel**

needed to hold the matt or artwork. A ³/₈ inch (10mm) rabbet is certainly enough for a matt used for an 8x10 photograph. What seems to work well is to have one or two strips which allow for the rabbet and project above a flat, broader middle piece and then to have several wider raised strips on the outside. Many frames have a 'narrowing' window in order to focus the viewer on the artwork and to prevent the eye from wandering.

Assembling

There are several approaches to assembling the carved strips. One is to carve the strips, then glue them into one board which is then mitred, rabbetted and assembled. This is the most direct way to make the frame. The individual strips are contiguous around the frame. One disadvantage is that the design

at the corner mitres might seem disjointed, having part of an increment awkwardly butting another. For example, half a bead may join a quarter of a bead thus having little straight walls interrupting the rounded forms. This may, depending on your aesthetic preferences, contribute to the zaniness of the piece. A second drawback to this method is that much carving is wasted in cutting the mitres. The frame in the picture on page 87 is, admittedly, a little more calculated than this cut-the-mitre-where-it-falls method.

The second approach is to glue up the various strips and mitre before carving, allowing each design to be calculated to work out nicely at the corners. This may destroy the random pleasure of creating something from practice pieces.

Above **Using a #9 to round beads**

Right **Carving a design into a flat surface**

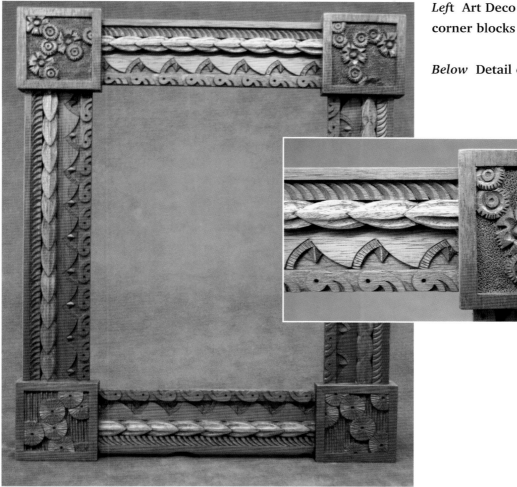

Left **Art Deco frame with corner blocks**

Below **Detail of corner block**

A third approach as shown above might be to avoid the whole mitre issue by having corner blocks to which the sides butt.

This allows you to cut the strips any length without the messiness of mis-matched increments. It also allows different profiles or a different order of the same profiles on different sides. That is, not contiguously running around the frame. The corner blocks should be slightly thicker than the profiles so that projecting profiles don't present a ragged appearance.

Some sort of decoration should break up the flat surface of the block. After carving, the sides should be glued together, trimmed and joined to the block with biscuits. The rabbets of the sides will have to be continued into the inner corner of the corner block so that the mat and artwork will lie well in the frame.

Needless to say the wood used should be chosen carefully so that there is colour match and that grain patterns don't draw attention to any disparity. Using two woods of contrasting colour might work well with a certain combination of designs, but this seems problematic and, besides, I think that the illusion that the frame members are 'from the solid' is something to promote. Staining will often even out colour differences.

Example: Rustic Frames

Left **The criss-cross frame showing theorem painting by Martha Wilbur**

When one thinks of picture frames, two extremes immediately come to mind: the heavily ornamented gilded frame of the eighteenth and nineteenth centuries and the simple wood moulded rectangle of the twentieth century, yet there was also a popular vernacular style known variously as Black Forest, criss-cross, Adirondack, or rustic frame (see how complicated it is!). The two frames described here are inspired by such a frame inherited from my grandfather, Lester Bliss Wilbur (1883–1973).

A similar style, the Victorian vernacular or Eastlake frame, commonly seen in antique shops and flea markets, is criss-cross in form, but having a water gilded sight edge and a triad of leaves applied at the corners, though I have seen flower and leaf arrangements as well. Though always 'factory carved' the form degenerated into dreadfully crude production frames with leaves simply cut out of flat stock or machine embossed.

The frame described first is carved to represent branches criss-crossed, ostensibly held together with nails and decorated with a pair of leaves. It is an intriguing idea to carve wood to appear as, well, wood – branches, twigs and knots. I have not seen another frame quite like this one, though I believe it is representative of this genre of frames. It reminds me of the Black Forest style of naturalistic carvings of bears on tree trunks or Victorian hunting trophies of pheasant and hunting horns. 'Rustic' is used here because of the intention – crossed sticks is hardly sophisticated style – and does not necessarily refer to crude technique.

Right **Antique rustic frame**

This frame is made of dressed mahogany stock, lap-jointed, cut in side profile and carved. The leaves at the top are the only reason this is a 'portrait' orientation as the four sides are configured exactly the same, with only modest dimensional stretch. I decided to rotate the new frame to a landscape orientation, thinking that the photographs I would likely frame would indeed be landscapes. Needless to say, the leaves are carved separately and literally nailed to the carved frame. The rabbet which holds the glass, mat and picture or photograph is stopped: that is, it was not made on lengths of stock before assembly as most mitre frames are made, the joint concealing and 'stopping' the rabbets. The carving of this frame was quickly done as though mass produced, though it is not obviously a factory piece. There are rough areas with noticeable tear-out, several puzzling design elements such as the S and C stabbing near the ends and several techniques which rely on surface scarring. Though the faces of the pieces are completely carved, no attempt was made to carve the sides which remain flat. The protruding twigs were added to the lengths of prepared stock.

After studying the original, I decided to tweak the perceived technique slightly to avoid its rough quality, so I took the 'in-the-style-of' approach which seemed the most judicious route. I did not copy every cut or mark. I observed that some of the twigs do not flow continuously from the branch, but were instead angled. I wanted them to curve outwardly with more grace. I did not dig deep grooves or the illogical S and C stabs on the extensions.

I wanted to enlarge the original frame's 10 (25.4cm) x 12 (30.5cm) inch rabbet accommodation to the 11(27.9cm) x 14 inch (35.6cm) standard mat which allows for an 8 x 10 photograph. (The actual opening is slightly smaller than 8 x 10 in order to cover the margins of the photograph). Unless you have an outdoor scene and the projecting twigs give some feeling of depth, they could be very distracting – a problem that using a mat eliminates. I did not, therefore, simply enlarge proportionally the smaller to the larger frame, though the ratios of the two frames are not hugely different. I began by drawing the mat size on a piece of drawing paper. From this 'given' I brought the 'window' inward a quarter inch to create the rabbet and decided that if the frame size was to be larger, the frame widths would be slightly larger as well. I did measure the extension of the branches past the corner on the original frame and guessed at the slight increase for the new frame. A similar procedure was used in the thickness of the frame members as well as the leaf arrangement. The thickness has to allow for the up-turned ends of the branches, so it may be advisable to draw a side elevation on one side of the four pieces. The lap joint has to be positioned toward the back of the bottom member so that when the front profile is cut the joint is not infringed upon.

After dressing the stock, make the lap joints on the table saw using either a dado blade or repeated cuts with a single blade. Stops, fences and safety equipment should make accurate joints. Having the long sides overlap the short sides retains the rectangular proportion as there is a 'nail' head in the middle of the crossing (see detail, right). Having the short sides overlapping the longer and having the interruption of the nail heads makes the short sides appear even shorter. The two adjacent members should be flush at the back of the frame. The next operation is to make the rabbet in the back. I used a router with a bearing guided rabbeting bit, cleaning the corners with a bench chisel. The rabbet should be deep enough (³⁄₈ inch, 10mm) for glass, mat, artwork and any backing cardboard planned. One could drop the piece onto the

table saw blade controlling the extent of the cut with stops, but I wouldn't recommend this method, even though I believe the original was done in this way.

Finally, band saw the front faces to create the up-turned ends. You may want to delay cutting the forward slope of the ends so that the pieces can be more securely held between bench dogs. The picture on page 95 shows the progression of machine operations. To these blanks glue the twigs onto the sides. I made the blocks long enough so that a graceful curve could be carved on the side and I allowed them to project above the face of the frame slightly.

The back of the inner twigs should be even with the step of the rabbet and the exterior ones should be similarly placed. After the glue is cured, use the band saw to cut the twig outlines.

Right **Details of original frame corner**

Carving

Secure the piece or pieces between bench dogs, in a vice or clamped to the bench top before beginning to carve. Begin carving by rounding the front edges of the pieces and removing the band saw marks on the faces using a shallow (#2 or #3) gouge. Fair the curve of the twigs into the branches. The upper lapped pieces have round 'nail' heads in the centre of the crossing, which does not want to be reduced by much. The crossing is the thickest area along the pieces.

Using a #10 or #11 (5mm) gouge, make a groove along the midline of the piece, then a groove parallel to the curve of the twig to define its up-tree edge.

Bevel the twig into the side of the branch and into the groove just created on the up-tree side so that there is a ridge curving along the midline of the twig. You may have to deepen the midline groove of the branch in order to have the twig stand out from the face of the branch. Don't worry about making the twigs absolutely round. On the opposite side of the branch from the twig is a bulge which will be the knot. This knot should have a peak and slope both up and down the tree.

On the two longer pieces, stab in circular nail heads and relieve them with a #8. The ends, which are sloping, are divided into semicircular rounds with a shallow gouge,

Left **Parts of the frame, showing the lap joint and the shape of the end**

Below **The twigs are glued on to the main pieces**

Left **Separating up-tree side of twigs**

Below **Further definition of twigs**

Bottom **Texturing the twigs with rocking motion**

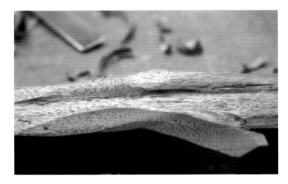

the same #2 previously used for rounding and cleaning band saw marks. At this point the forming of the elements is complete, and what remains is surface texturing.

One characteristic of the original frame is the scarring technique of the twigs by 'walking' a #5 gouge down the sloping surfaces of the twig. Place the gouge with the in-cannel toward the downward slope and very gently make an impression. Relieving the pressure, but without lifting the gouge, one wing of the blade is pivoted a short way down the twig, then the other wing, and so forth down the twig a little passed where it joins the main branch.

You should practice this continuous rocking motion technique on scrap wood several times. There may be slight tear-out; the steeper the slope the less this occurs. The branch-ends which curve outward are easier to do than the twigs, though a slightly wider gouge (8mm #5) is used. Another unusual technique used on the

original is in making the multiple steps leading away from the protruding knot. It appears as though a gouge, turned over, was simply stabbed at an angle and the wood split away. Again, on a steep enough slope this is easier, but some of the mess is avoided by first stabbing-in a series of curves and then relieving them with the same gouge. The entire surface of the pieces

Right **The process of texturing the knot**

Below right **Main branch bark is carved**

Below **Back-cutting the twigs while held in a vice**

is grooved with the #10 (or #11) in irregularly parallel lines. There are several places where the grooves curve over the sides or along the twig. The pieces are turned over and the twigs are back-cut to thin them. In re-gluing one twig of the original frame, I noticed that several others

had been re-attached as well, so I decided to make the new ones with more glue surface. This means a little more material had to be carved at the ends in order to make the twig more round as shown in the picture left.

The up-turned ends are also back-cut and somewhat rounded, though again the sides were flat as on the original. It is best to hold these pieces vertically in a vice to carve them. The ends were made concave so that from the front view they have more interest than if left flat. The sloped ends have a circle made with #10 or #11 and the pith indicated by stabbing the #8 gouge and

relieving on the front side. After the frame is glued, the back of the joints are relieved so they don't look so thick when viewed from the side.

On a ½ inch (13mm) thick piece of stock trace the arrangement of leaves and band saw or scroll saw the silhouette. Use the paper and glue method of holding the blank while carving. The applied leaves are modelled with ridges between the lobes of the leaves, one overlapping the other. The stem is sloped quickly at the ends to simulate the tear or cut of the pair from

Top **The branch end**

Left **Using the glue and paper method of securing the blank**

Below **Pattern for leaf appliqué**

APPLIQUÉ LEAF TEMPLATE

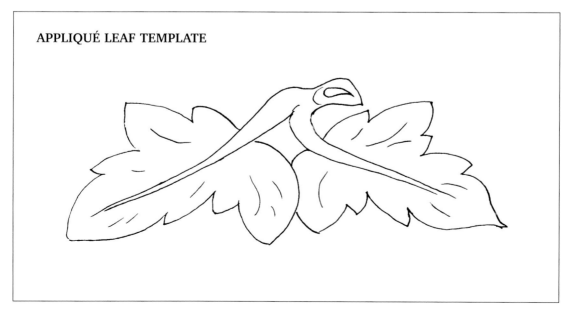

a branch and some texture is added using the same gouge rocking technique as on the twigs. The original leaves are simply tacked on with small cut nails, there being no flat surface upon which to glue them. A small brad with head hammered to a square looks authentic enough. I sanded the flat surfaces and used 0000 extra fine steel wool over the entire surface to remove fuzz and soften the surface. I finished with a dark stain and wax trying to replicate the original colour.

The asphaltum/varnish mix could also have been used to this effect.

Above **The completed appliqué**

Below **The completed frame with appliqué**

Left **The completed frame**

Inspired by the replication of the rustic frame just described, I thought that a frame with rope-lashed branches with twigs carved from the solid might be interesting. It would certainly complement the batik of the herons I intended to frame. When finished, this frame reminded me of Black Forest carvings sans bear. The term Black Forest style seems to be a popular genre for the collector these days as the label is frequently encountered on auction website item descriptions and there are also antiques sites with lots of items. Trouble is, Black Forest (after a location in Germany) is a grand misnomer as the carving to which it refers was actually produced in Brienz, Switzerland and environs (see bibliography). Extremely popular in the last quarter of the nineteenth century, the style depicts hunting motifs of pheasants, bears, rabbits, foxes and the hounds which hunt them. These animals are often lurking in vegetation and thus oak leaves and wild grape vines are often used. Much of the carving was 'factory' carved, meaning that shops produce prodigious numbers of carvings for the tourist trade. Consequently, the animals are quickly shaped and then 'textured' fur or feathers are efficiently done. The result is not the photographic realism so admired today, but none the less a naturalistic treatment.

As before, I lap jointed the four sides and rabbeted the interior back edges to accept the artwork, the mat and the glass. The width of the stock should be wider than the intended finished width because the lashings require width in the 90 degree corner on all four interstices; see the picture above.

Because the sides of the stock are reduced in width, the rabbet is cut further into the edge to compensate for this reduction of the rabbet. I glued the frame before commencing to rout the rabbet.

Above **Layout of the corner lashings**

I decided to carve the lashings first because I thought they would prove more challenging, but also to establish the width of the branches. I proceeded to bost, set-in and relieve the X of the lashings. Because the branches are rounded and the lashings are as well, I began to round

Below **Setting-in of the lashings**

both, simultaneously extending the limits of the lashing down each corner, as shown below. You have to carve the branches down a significant amount in order to have the lashing arrive at the back of the stock without a machined corner down its middle. The orientation of the grain and the shortness of material as it butts the crosspiece increases the probability of splitting off a small triangular piece (especially if the joint wasn't tightly made). Clamping the frame in a vice may provide better access. In this position a knife may be useful to help define or separate the lashings from the branch.

Decide how the lashings will overlap each other and then draw the individual strands. Having one strand 'underlap' (as it were) the parallel strands adds verisimilitude and interest. See below right.

Left **Extending the lashing down the four interior corners**

Below Left **Using a knife to clean interior corners**

Below Right **The completed lashing**

Above **Backside view**

Above **A stop-cut allows for rounding the main branches**

Above **Separating the twigs further from the main branches**

Right **Rounding twig ends**

Far right **Clearing-up around twigs**

The strands can be made by a parting tool or set-in with chisel and then rounded. Of course the strands should wrap around to the back of the stock.

The reduction in width and thickness of the stock in producing the corner lashings has left material in the middle of the branches for the projecting twigs. Begin isolating the twigs by a groove roughly following the up-tree side, see picture middle left, and then, making a stop cut, round the branch on the up-tree side.

Next, define the down-tree sweep of the twigs beginning from the extremity and working down-tree, as illustrated in the picture (third bottom left). The end of the twig is angled and then undercut. On the angled twig end redraw the circular section of the cut off twig; round the twig and undercut so that the circular end is formed. Clean up around the back side of the twig (below, left). What is left to do is to texturize the surfaces to mimic bark, knots and end grain. A small veiner is used to create the 'flow' of the bark. The veiner

Above **Making the knot and texturizing the main branches**

Above **Carving the end grain pith and rings with a #8**

leaves a softer appearance than a parting tool. You should plan several vesica piscus shaped areas in which to place knots. These, of course, could be done first and then the texture carved around them.

The knots are simply small circulate depressions made with a small #9 or possibly just punched. Several crescent shaped cuts are made with a #8, stabbed in and slightly relieved. These knots should bulge slightly from the surrounding texture, but this is nothing to fiddle around about. Next bevel the branch end, with a slight curve. They should not necessarily be regular. The end grain 'growth rings' of the twigs are represented by an arc roughly following the circumference of the twig, while the larger branch ends require several of these rings, they also need pith. The pith is easily indicated by stabbing in a circle with a #8, the same gouge as used for the knots and relieving it on one side.

You shouldn't have to sand this piece at all upon completion of carving, but a scotch pad or fine steel wool will remove any fuzziness. The picture (below right) shows a detail of the corner. To finish, use the asphaltum varnish concoction previously described or a dark stain.

Below **The completed corner**

Right **Black Forest oak leaf frame**

The picture above shows another rustic frame in the Black Forest style, consisting of branches of oak leaves. It is not in as high relief or as flamboyant as some of the Swiss carved work, but does achieve some relief by the sloping ground; when viewed straight on the leaves are contained by the width of the frame, but when viewed at an angle the leaves break the hard straight line. Though there is a vertical orientation to the side members, the branch threading through the leaves is continuous. In spite of this, there is an internal logic to the design. Generally, such internal logic seems necessary for a successful carving, especially of a naturalistic subject. This frame has a stippled or punched ground. Introduced earlier, the technique of punching or stippling is used to add contrast between the ground and the smooth surfaces of the object in relief. By stippling the ground many small shadows are created, darkening it, while smooth surfaces reflect light and appear lighter. The technique can be misused in an attempt to cover poor grounding or gouge stab marks. Also, it is often done with impatience and detracts from the attractiveness of the piece. Not all carvings should be stippled. Alto-relievo naturally has more shadow and, therefore, more contrast than the several varieties of basso-relievo. With an application of finish, especially the penetrating oils, the stippling 'pops' out on most species of wood. A different purpose to punching is when punches are used to clarify certain small recesses such as circular holes and 'eyes' between lobes of foliage (the classical acanthus leaf is an example) or other small recesses such as the triangular space between grapes in a cluster.

Commercially made punches are available from supply houses and sets of pointed ones, both square and round in section, are extremely useful for most situations. There are also punches with designs of stars, flowers, acorns and so forth, but these have extremely limited application. The box on page 115 has been stamped with a flower punch, but it is difficult to make even impressions. You can make punches from odd bits of bar stock, metal rods, bolts and cut or hardened nails.

You should strive to stipple evenly and, because it is difficult to do this with a multi-toothed punch, you should overlap the punches so that the surface is evenly dimpled. The surface should look like sandpaper without flat areas between dimples. It means a lot of hammering and finger fatigue, but worth it in the effectiveness of readability. It seems logical to do broad areas with the punches with the most teeth whether square or round, and then work into the smaller areas with smaller tools, making final dimples in acute spaces or undercuts with a single pointed tool. Stippling the entire surface with a single sharp round point made from a nail, for instance, creates a subtly different texture from the multi-toothed punch, the teeth of the punch being pyramids and not conical points.

Below **Detail of the oak leaves frame**

Above **Completed Florentine frame with pierced leaf design**

The design for this frame derives from an illustration in *A Manual of Traditional Wood Carving*, labelled as a Florentine frame. I have been unable to determine whether this designation is based on stylistic characteristics or for some other reason. It has a scrolled and pierced leaf design. Pierced carvings are common in architecture, furniture, as well as accessories, most notably in the Gothic decorations of tracery, crestings and mouldings. The idea that the frame itself can be looked through is a kind of irony, especially if one takes a frame as a 'window' one looks through to 'see' the world depicted in the artwork held within.

At any rate, pierced carvings are always intriguing whether a lattice-like depiction or voids within a more sculptural piece, because of the interplay of light and shadow and form and void or **negative space**. This technique begins with the design. In designing, there should be some thought given to the balance of positive to negative space with some attention to their distribution. You have to consider the stability or fragility of the wood itself; the design should provide connection or overlap of elements. This type of carving, then, is not simply removing the

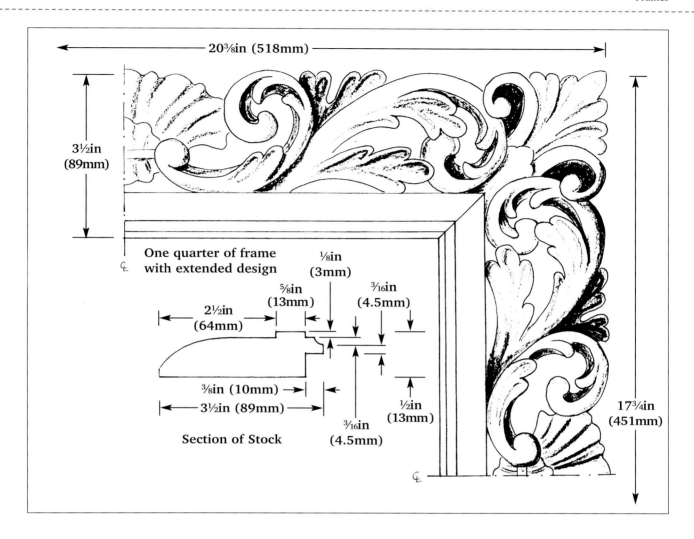

20⅜in (518mm)

3½in (89mm)

One quarter of frame with extended design

⅛in (3mm)

⅝in (13mm)

³⁄₁₆in (4.5mm)

2½in (64mm)

³⁄₈in (10mm)

3½in (89mm)

³⁄₁₆in (4.5mm)

½in (13mm)

Section of Stock

17¾in (451mm)

ground of an otherwise usual relief carving. But conversely, most pierced carvings could be relief carvings with a ground. Because the carved area of this frame has a curved profile, the design will need to be extended from what is depicted on the flat or elevation drawing. The carved area here is 2½ inches (64mm) in the elevation (face) drawing, but needs to widened ⅛-¼ inch (3-6mm) to extend the width of the actual blank.

With this frame the four sides are essentially the same design, though, of course, altered to fit the different lengths. Much of the difference can be made up in the middle 'shell'

Above **Drawing showing half of each side**

ornament. The leaves at the mitres should be symmetrical as corners tend to be visual reference points. The drawing represents half of each side and indeed the most efficient method of design is to figure out one half of each side and to replicate its mirror image. This can be done either by folding along the centre line and taping the paper up to a window (or light box) and tracing through the paper or by using a separate piece of tracing paper and flipping it over the centre line to transfer the design to the other side.

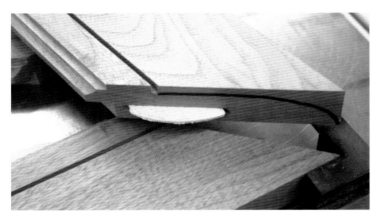

Above **End view shows the section and saw kerf separating band from the carved area**

Right **Hand plane the curve. Note the sample piece**

Two methods

There are two conceivable methods for producing pierced carvings. The first and probably the most common is to drill and saw out the spaces before carving. The advantage of this method is that much material can be removed through efficient mechanical means. The disadvantage, at least in this case, is that the curved profile creates the potential for cutting elements too closely so that when carved they are not true to the layout. The spaces here are fairly small so using a scroll saw is laborious and a sabre saw is unsatisfactory.

The second method is to carve the elements with deep recesses which, when material is taken from the back, breaks through to the recesses, creating the open space. This provides for a substantial substrate to stabilize the work when carving delicate or fragile detail. This is the method Grinling Gibbons used to carve the lace of his famous Walpole cravat. In this situation, I drilled holes on the drill press through those areas perpendicular to the drill and did not attempt to saw the spaces. I used a portable drill to drill perpendicular to the surface of the profile for holes on the curve.

Much Italian Renaissance woodwork including cassoni, frames, and furniture were made of walnut (*Juglans regia*), and so I have followed that notion by using American black walnut. I have found that aired dried walnut is very pleasant wood to carve. It has a much richer colour than the steam-dried walnut offered by most suppliers. It also has a superb balance of hardness and softness lacking in many hardwoods.

Dimension

Consult the drawing and then dress and dimension the material. On the table saw cut the rabbet. As mentioned above, if working to a pre-determined size, such as a standard mat, the width of the rabbet should be determined first and appropriate measurements taken from the inner wall. Next, make a 'step' on the face side wide enough to be able to rout a cove into it. See the section drawing on page 107. If the bearing of your cove bit will not have enough side surface against which to ride, you may want to do this edge before cutting the rabbet. Next, separate the area to be carved from the flat band with a $\frac{1}{8}$ inch (3mm) deep saw kerf.

You can remove a small amount ($\frac{1}{8}$ inch) from the surface to be carved, saving a little planning time later. Though it seems logical to make the profile for the carving before cutting the mitres, this presents the problem of uneven clamping while gluing, pressure being exerted only on one edge of the pieces. I have always favoured mechanical joints so

Above **Drill the blank with portable drill**

Right **Setting-in, enlarging the holes to conform to the setting-in of outline**

I recommend using splines or biscuits at the mitred corners. Locate the biscuit toward the back of the mitre. Glue the four sides together. As above, a table saw may be used to bevel the outer edge to reduce the planning of the desired profile. Hand plane the angles, and you are very close to the desired curve. Allow enough material at the edge to accommodate the curved scroll. Transfer the design to the profiled frame, marking the spaces with an X. Cut the outside silhouette on a band saw, a scroll saw or copping saw. As with any such cutting of the silhouette, this operation will determine the shape of the carved element, so make sure the design is accurately transferred or cut slightly wide of the mark to allow for adjustment. Because of the overlap of scrolls at the corners enough material must be left so undercutting doesn't leave one too thin.

Drill various sized holes in the areas of void. This procedure gives definition to the negative and positive spaces and serves as bosting or wasting to the 'outside' of the lines.

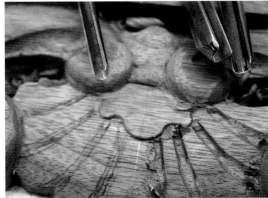

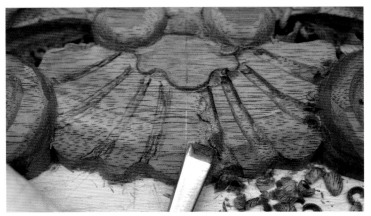

Top left **Scrolls with internal leaflets. The convex/concave nature of the scroll**

Top right **The grooves of the shell are started with a deep gouge**

Left **The convex areas are rounded with #3 gouge**

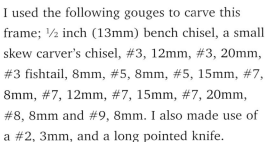

I used the following gouges to carve this frame; ½ inch (13mm) bench chisel, a small skew carver's chisel, #3, 12mm, #3, 20mm, #3 fishtail, 8mm, #5, 8mm, #5, 15mm, #7, 8mm, #7, 12mm, #7, 15mm, #7, 20mm, #8, 8mm and #9, 8mm. I also made use of a #2, 3mm, and a long pointed knife.

Carving

Secure the blank on the bench. It might be advisable to have a scrap piece of plywood behind the blank so that stabbing cuts which penetrate the spaces don't mar the bench or mount to the work station by screwing through the plywood to secure from behind. Carve the elements as in any relief carving, setting-in the outlines and then modelling the surfaces. Stab in the outlines of the scrolls and

leaves, matching tool sweep to line. In walnut, a smart tap with a mallet will do for much of the setting-in, especially in the shallow areas at the corners (remember those hidden biscuits!). There is not much need or, indeed, opportunity to bost-in. I often follow the setting-in of long curves (having used a wide gouge) with smaller width gouges, especially when there is little clearance between elements. These smaller gouges have to be of a shallower sweep in order to match the original curve.

Continue to define the negative space, but don't worry about absolute clarity in the acute corners which are much easier to clean after the material is thinned by back cutting. Also, keep away from the straight inner wall of the frame as this will be shaved smooth later.

Right **The frame is secured on padding for back-cutting, note the rolled padding at right to support the frame edge**

Continue carving by differentiating layers and overlaps. There are a number of overlaps: several leaflets of the 'top' layer of scrolling foliage, the corner leaves overlapping itself and the scrolling foliage, the scrolling foliage overlapping the shell and the 'background' leaves in the V between the oppositely scrolling leaves. Relieve around such top level elements and lower the 'background' leaves between the two scrolls of foliage.

There are several scrolls at the corners as well as those at the centre shell. They can be set-in with #7s and #5. As in customary C and S scrolls, the outer part of the form is convex while the inner part is concave. This can be done with a small #3 or medium #5 gouge turned over. At the 'eye' of the scroll a #7 can be used to create the cove by a steep relieving cut, but on most of the scroll a #8 will form a nice deep cove. These scrolls have 'internal' leaflets which should also be differentiated by a concave profile (see picture top left of p110). The convex areas touching the perpendicular inner wall of the flat band are deeply sloped into it. Set-in the smaller leaflets with the #8 or #9 gouge.

It is a little hard to decipher what is intended by the centre ornament from the drawing in *Manual of Traditional Wood Carving*; it is not really a shell, but it could be a fan of fabric. I did not literally make a shell, but treated it more abstractly. I have noticed from time to time in observing wood carved decoration, a curious mix of the naturalistic and the abstract or geometric. As with shells, the indentation of the silhouette usually indicates a surface groove so I have followed this convention. Because the surface should undulate, turn over a #3 gouge and round the convex surfaces.

Leave the carving of the corner leaflets and the background leaves of the sides until you have finished the back-cutting as the eventual thin sections may be damaged in the next process. Turn the frame over and secure it using fences, and padding and begin the process of **back-**

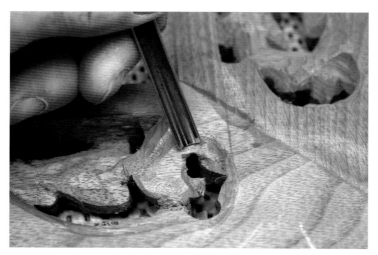

Left **Using a #9 gouge to back-cut near the biscuit joint**

lending a lightness to the foliage. On a curved and pierced carving the viewer is able to see the edges of the elements. Not all the material needs to be taken away, but enough to have the edges of the elements appear somewhat thin. You will find that you are frequently turning the frame over to check your progress from the front side; marking areas for further removal is done with chalk or white pencil. Back-cutting this frame will take some time and though it doesn't seem as 'sexy' as carving the front curlicues, care must be taken not to break thin sections.

cutting. A piece of rug pad rolled and held with rubber bands can be placed under the edge to keep the frame from tipping. Back-cutting involves accentuating the face side overlaps, and to thin the material thus

Below **Clamp in a vice for access to edges**

The hardest areas are those of small spaces and close to where the biscuit is hidden. Use a #8 or #9 gouge to back cut these areas.

Clean-up especially of acute angles can be achieved by using a pointed knife, but be careful not to poke your fingers when the blade penetrates the hole. There is no need to create a *tour de force* and attempt to make the entire piece thin, but leaving material retains strength.

Return to the front side and clean the vertical wall, making sure machine marks are carved out and the approach from the back matches the front. You may want to clamp the frame vertically in a bench vice to access the edge scrolls.

If there are pressure marks from your tools along the arris of the vertical wall, wetting this area will reduce the need for sanding these nicks out.

I used a stiff brush to reduce the remaining fuzz from crevices and then lightly sanded, followed by 0000 fine steel wool. You can purchase oil-free steel wool from finishing suppliers, but I rarely have problems in using ordinary steel wool. As for finish, this air dried walnut is rich by itself, needing only an oil finish.

Choosing a light coloured mat (for a photograph) makes the walnut appear darker. If the art work to be framed is itself somewhat dark, the sight edge cove could be gilded.

Below **Detail of finished carving**

"... take pains and pleasure in constantly copying the best things which you can find done by the hand of great masters."

Cennini, *Il Libro dell'Arte*

Chapter Five

Boxes

◆ **Unlidded containers** ◆ **Waste basket** ◆ **Tray** ◆ **Jewellery box** ◆ **CD cabinet**

In a sense most of the projects in this book are containers – bookracks, picture frames, etc, but in this chapter I stay closer to the common box. Boxes are of all configurations and made from many different materials; from hollowed out logs to cloisonné reliquaries, stone sarcophagi to papier-mache portable desks and the ubiquitous plastic packaging of contemporary life.

Boxes of wood can be strictly utilitarian crates with nailed butt joints or a 'work of art' with meticulously cut dovetails and inlaid or carved surfaces. And, of course, they can be filled with cultural and religious meaning.

There are, of course, many kinds of wood containers – split oak baskets, turned vessels, and coopered pails and barrels, speciality containers for tea, sewing notions and scientific instruments. One usually thinks of boxes as essentially rectangular and made of assembled pieces. But boxes can be made by bending, as in oval Shaker boxes and the 'kerf-bent' boxes of the Native Americans of the Northwest Coast; or by hollowing out a solid block of wood, as in band sawn boxes. They may be multi-sided (up to the point it becomes a barrel!) or turned. 'Bins' usually don't have tops, but boxes generally have lids. Here, of course, the emphasis will be on the decoration of the usual box form.

Design

The first design consideration is the purpose or use of the planned container which naturally requires some thought about size, shape or other special features (such as handling, internal compartments, the need to lock the lid and so on). After these basic parameters have been decided, construction needs to be considered. There are a number of joints which can be used and a good book to consult is *Taunton's Complete Illustrated Guide to Box Making* by Doug Stowe. Many

Left **Box with lap joint**

Above **Nails are integrated into the design**

books on furniture construction have explanations of 'box' joints. Though it is tempting to plan for fancy visible joints such as dovetails, finger joints and keyed mitre joints, these construction details may detract or, indeed, interfere with the carving. In fact, the original instructions for the jewellery box explained below, indicate that the dovetails should be covered with a plain pilaster block. (See *A Manual of Traditional Wood Carving, page 224*).

The simplest corner joint is a butt joint which is nailed or screwed, but this construction also presents a visual distraction by having exposed end grain patterns when the grain is oriented horizontally. This may be off-set somewhat by a carved edge treatment as previously illustrated. (See Chapter Three.) Fasteners, such as nails or screws, could be incorporated into the design. The box

pictured on page 115 has an end-grain lap joint held with glue and copper nails. Notice the detail in the picture above. A butt joint along the grain avoids this difference in grain patterns and is a stronger glue joint. This is practical for taller boxes such as the utensil boxes explained below.

The best joint from a carver's point of view is one which does not detract from the carving! Generally, this is taken to mean those which do not show any end grain. There is the common mitre (held with biscuits or internal splines), the lock mitre and the hidden dovetail mitre. For our purposes the biscuit joined or splined mitre will be easiest to construct and assemble. It is certainly strong enough for the items made here.

Example: Unlidded Containers

The open boxes here and on page 120 are intended for storing kitchen utensils. One has a horizontal design while the second a vertical one. The vine works well in situations that continue around the form as it pulls the eye along. Designs on turned forms naturally do this. A horizontal band wrapped around the vertical form can create an interesting tension. Interrupting the verticality of form can also change our perception of the height of the piece. Virginia creeper (*Parthenocissus quinquefolia*) is an interesting vine, having five leaflets radiating from a central stem. From a practical design standpoint, the leaves can be rotated to fit a predetermined space and do not necessarily have to be visually attached to the main vine. The berries add a contrasting shape and punctuate the spaces between leaves. The leaflets are ovoid with pointed ends and irregularly toothed edges.

Instead of stylizing the vine and cramming it into a strict space, having the leaflet tips and berries 'breaking' the borders

Below **Virginia creeper vine. The vertical lines indicate the corners of the box**

Above **Kitchen utensil box**

of the band gives it a naturalistic feel. In the drawing below, the design is not a naturally depicted Virginia creeper vine because there is no overlap of leaves, no perspective, no modelling indicated, but is instead a line drawing. The vine in nature is airy with

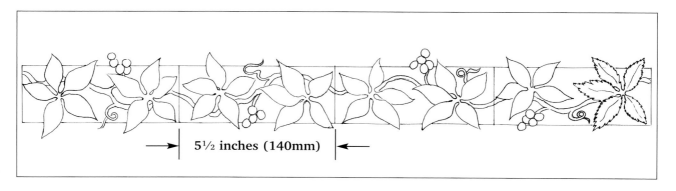

5½ inches (140mm)

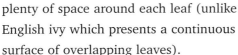

Top left **A magnifying lamp with light is useful for incising work**

Above **Lamp holding bench dog**

Left **Use short angled cuts to tooth the edges of the leaf**

plenty of space around each leaf (unlike English ivy which presents a continuous surface of overlapping leaves).

As you design for woodcarving, it is reasonable to have in mind the technique to be used to accomplish the design in the material. The incised technique, described earlier, does not easily allow for complicated overlaps of leaves as this would prove to be visually confusing. The depiction on this box is uncomplicated with few instances of three-dimensionality and, because it is etched into the surface, is more subtle than the second instance below which has more relief producing more shadows. (It also has a contrast in colour between carving and surrounding surface.)

Decide on the placement and width of the background band. Then, mechanically draw it and indicate where the design will wrap around the box. I used 2 inch (51mm) for the width on the 12 inch (305mm) tall box and 22 inch (558mm) to wrap around the 5 ½ inches

(140mm) box. Place tracing paper over it and proceed to design a vine which runs around the corners, each side having a different placement of leaves, berries and tendrils. On this example the sides are 5½ inches (140mm) wide so two leaves and a bunch of berries fill the space nicely. It is visually difficult to 'bend' leaves around a 90 degree corner. You don't have to draw all the toothed edges, but the five ovoid leaves are all that is necessary. The berries shouldn't be located in the same position of each side, nor should the leaves be placed on the horizontal centre line. There should be some balance to the border overlaps.

This design can be incised using a #15, (45 degree), 4mm parting tool, a #12 (60 degree) parting tool, 6mm, a #9, 5mm gouge and a #11, 3mm veiner. Though there are few tools used for this design, care must be taken to have them sharp. The parting tools should effortlessly change direction in the wood. Of course, you must select wood which is amenable to the incised technique,

such as walnut, soft maple, cherry or mahogany. These two utensil boxes have biscuit joined mitred sides.

To transfer the design, graphite on the back of a sheet of paper is better than the traditional carbon paper because the lines left by the latter are difficult to erase, and you shouldn't sand the shallow relief after carving.

Because the incised lines are so shallow, a slanting light is advantageous to keeping track of the progress of the parting tool. A magnifying lamp might also prove helpful. Any desk lamp having a pin which fits into a mounting block can be used. A wooden block fitted with a peg similar in size to a bench dog can be drilled to accommodate the pin of the lamp and is, therefore, adjustable along the bench. Begin incising the leaves with the #15 parting tool by starting at the tip and, more or less following the ovoid outline, make the toothed edge of the leaflet with small angled cuts. The cuts following the

Top **Centre vein is deeper and wider**

Centre **The background is a series of parallel flutes**

Above **The design wraps around the delicate mitre joint**

Left **Detail of the incised vine**

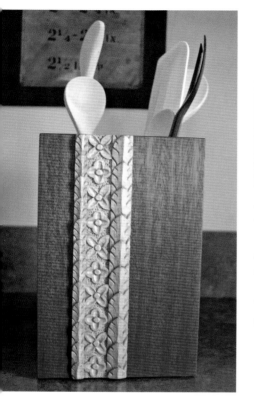

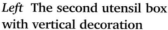

Left **The second utensil box with vertical decoration**

Above **Separate strips are carved and glued together**

Top right **Detail of the second side**

ovoid outline are longer than the angled 'inner' ones. Put a slight inward curve to the longer lines. The spikes should not be too regular (as might be made for an apple, cherry, or apricot leaf). Continue incising the tendrils, berries and vine. The general depth of these incised lines is $\frac{1}{32}$ or $\frac{1}{16}$ of an inch, just one or two millimetres.

Next, with the #12 describe the straight lines of the background and the centre vein of the leaflets. This will be a wider valley. The smaller veins of the leaves are done with the #15. The straight lines of the border should be deeper than the other lines of the design. The background is textured by parallel grooves made by the #9 gouge. These should not be mechanical looking, having random regularity of depth and parallelism. Begin at the leaf edges and work toward the background space; approach

from the mitred corners toward the design as the mitred corners, even with a tight glue joint, are delicate. The small #11 veiner is used to clear the space between the steams of the leaflets. A stiff brush will likely remove most clinging chips.

With most incised work, some way to highlight the design is necessary. The most expedient way is to stain the piece with traditional stains, asphaltum as previously described, or a pigmented Danish oil. A moisture resistant finish can also be applied as the utensil holder will get kitchen splatter and moisture from washed utensils. In fact, small holes could be drilled in the bottom for additional air circulation.

The second utensil holder is the same size and construction as the first, but the decoration is oriented vertically. It is made of separately carved strips. The strips are glued together and then let into the sides of the box. I made each side of similar but different designs, compare the pictures top left and right. I used the sapwood of walnut culls as a light coloured wood to contrast with the darker mahogany though the carving relies less on the profile of the material as in earlier projects than on set-in and grounded repeats. The recess was made with a dado blade on the table saw.

Left **A box as a waste basket or planter**

The waste basket or planter box introduces sloped sides and larger surfaces on which to carve more intricate designs. 'Traditional' does not necessarily denote low-tech construction as this example demands accurate machining and patience in assembly. If you plan to use this as a waste basket you may want to alter the dimensions to accept a small shredder; if for a planter you may want to drill some holes in the bottom and add thin spacer feet to allow for drainage.

As with several other projects in this book, the design for this waste basket or planter is taken from an old carving manual. In older publications the illustrations and photographs are not always captioned, dimensioned or clear enough to create immediately a design of your own. Frequently, you will have to extrapolate your dimensions from a drawing or photograph and unless you are attempting a verbatim reproduction, an educated guess or your own sizing preferences will get you going. Serious reproduction furniture makers examine the construction, material, finish, hardware and so on of the original and measure the minutest detail.

Those of us who lean toward the 'in-the-style-of' school can adapt illustrated designs to our needs and preferences. The waste basket here is not dimensioned in the original text or drawing so you have to inject your own measurements.

Extrapolating

Most line drawings showing furniture or accessories are presented either straight-on (an elevation) or show two sides at once. The failure of the first is that the other sides of the object are completely hidden, requiring additional drawings for clarity and completeness. An elevation is, however, a faithful representation of the surface dimensions and pictorial design.

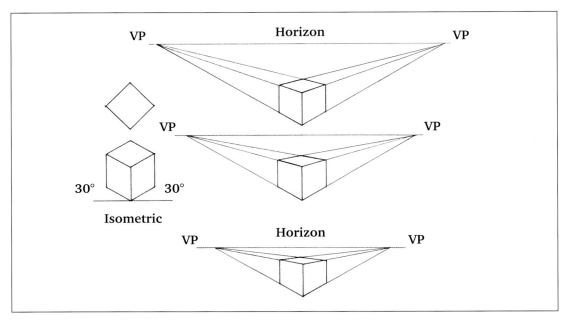

The three dimensional representation is either a conventionalized isometric drawing or a perspective drawing or photograph. Both views distort the actual object represented. These representations, however, have the advantage of showing multiple sides and their relationships. Photographs of furniture are often taken from an angle and, of course, distortion is introduced.

In both methods there is a 'forward' corner or what we'll call the Primary Vertical, from which the two visible sides of the object extend 'backward'. Assuming the object is sitting on a flat, level surface and is a cube or rectangle, comparing this centre vertical to the 'back' ones determines which convention was used. If they are the same measure, the **isometric** view (or isometric projection) was used, while a smaller 'back' vertical indicates the use of **perspective** to represent the object. As the term suggests, an isometric view is drawn such that both sides and top are shown equally as illustrated in the drawing above.

Above **Comparison of isometric and perspective views**

Using the Primary Vertical as a perpendicular or a front corner, draw a base line at the lower end of this vertical. Assuming that the cube or object has a 90 degree corner, extend the sides away from the corner at 30 degree angles. All edges (arrises) are then drawn parallel to these lower edges. You will notice in this example, using a cube, that two sides and the top are the same (congruent) rhomboid. This is generally the most useful representation of an object for the purposes of visualizing relationships and construction details.

The second method of representation, perspective, is considered more true to visual reality in spite of the graphic distortion. Simply stated, perspective is the visual phenomenon which accounts for objects further from the eye appearing smaller than those closer. The classic example is of railroad tracks – always parallel in reality but appearing to converge on the horizon. In fact, the fence and trees along the tracks converge at the same **vanishing point**. However, in the case of a cube or rectilinear furniture with a vertical defining the angle of two planes (sides) each plane diminishes toward its own vanishing point. See the drawing on page 122. Photography – film or digital – mimics this phenomenon so pictures of objects or furniture must be treated as perspective views no matter how slight the phenomenon may seem.

To extrapolate usable views (dimensional relationships) of the waste basket or planter, you have first to determine that it is an isometric view. Drawing a base line perpendicular to the centre vertical and measuring the angles on either side to the bottom edge of the illustration determines that it is an isometric view, each angle being 30 degrees. Measuring the width of the two sides, and the fact that the shape of the top is a rhombus, allows you to conclude that the waste basket is square.

To draw the plan and elevation of the waste basket, photocopy the illustration and mount it to a larger sheet of paper (cutting the illustration out and photocopying on a larger piece of paper works well). Dropping lines from the extremities of the object

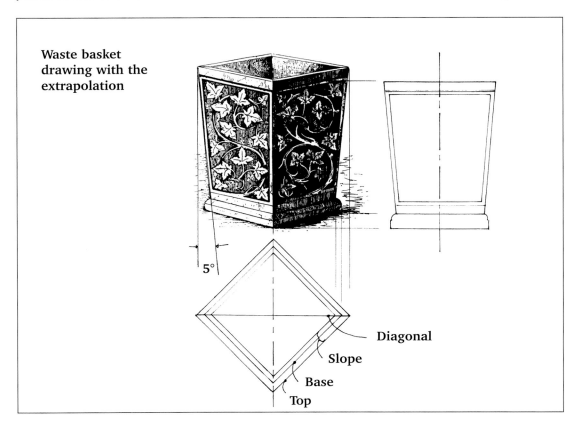

Waste basket drawing with the extrapolation

5°

Diagonal

Slope

Base

Top

determines the diagonal measurement of the square plan. The diagonals on the base and at the top of the plinth moulding are also found in this way. The intersections of these lines should coincide with the primary vertical or centre line. The measurement of the sides of the square, as constructed on the plan view, are used to mark out widths on the elevation which is drawn next.

The primary vertical is used as a 'story pole' because each division or element (rails, drawers, mouldings, and hardware on furniture) is in a true proportion to the whole so it can be extended horizontally, parallel to the base line to create the vertical measurements of the elevation. Any point on the surface, in fact, can be transferred to the elevation by extending a line parallel to the edges of the object to the primary vertical and thence, to the elevation. The widths are derived by measuring the sides as represented in the plan drawing.

Similar methods can be used on a photograph in which perspective comes into play. Perspective implies distance, but with smaller objects the discrepancies are not great. If you are interested in pursuing the complex subject (sloping planes, looking up or down on an object, laying out repeating shapes) there are books available on the subject – see the bibliography). If the viewer is looking directly at the corner of the object and both sides angle the same from the baseline, the perspective is symmetrical and the vanishing points of the sides are equidistant from the primary vertical. Measuring the two sides will determine whether the object is square or rectilinear. But such a neat situation is uncommon. Most photographs emphasize the front over the side so the perspective has vanishing points at different distances from the primary vertical. I imagine there is a geometrical method to determine the plan and, therefore, measurements of the object in a photograph, but in reality this procedure is difficult to perform because the vanishing points are often several feet from the photograph and the necessary constructions are unwieldy. Fortunately, 'specimen' photographs from museums or furniture books often supply overall dimensions so elevations can be made by extending horizontal lines and plugging in the appropriate widths and depth measurements after converting them to the scale of the primary vertical.

After drawing the elevation or plan, the same size as the book illustration or photograph, you will need to 'up-scale' to the actual size you will be carving. If the height of the piece is to be X and the literal measurement of the primary vertical of the illustration or photograph is Y divide X by Y and arrive at a ratio of X to Y. This translation factor holds for any comparable measurements from illustration or photograph to full sized drawing. I have found that it is easier to measure the small photograph or illustration in millimetres.

For example, I decided the waste basket was to be 305 millimetres (twelve inches) tall. I measured the illustration height at 85mm, so divided 305mm by 85mm to arrive at the ratio of 3.58 (the real thing is three and a half times the picture in the book). So multiplying all illustration measurements by 3.58 gave me the up-scaled dimensions of the sides, plinth height, and the placement of the carved area in millimetres. If you are working (thinking) in imperial measurements you will need to convert millimetres to inches (divide millimetres by 2.5 to find inches). Obviously, you have to be consistent in using either imperial or metric measurements.

Above left Material is cut on the table saw

Above The assembly is easier with jigs and frame clamp

Left Blank secured in work station

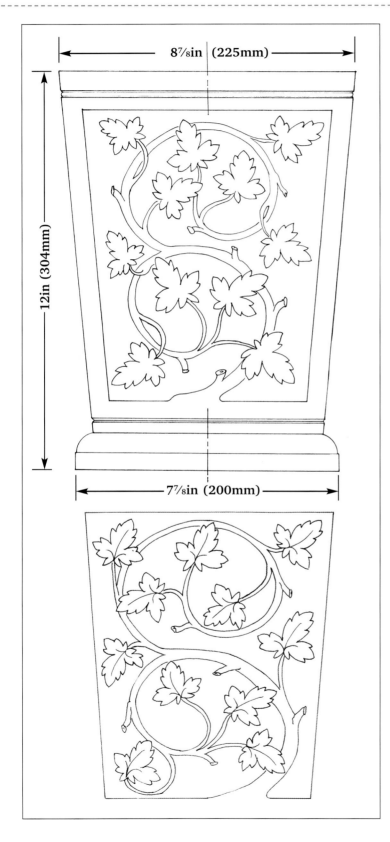

8⅞in (225mm)

12in (304mm)

7⅞in (200mm)

Left **Design of the waste basket**

To construct this waste basket or planter, dress the four sides identically and make the long dimension ⅛ inch (3mm) longer to allow for trimming after assembly. Set the table saw mitre gauge to five degrees. An auxiliary fence is attached to the mitre gauge to safely support the pieces. The blade should be tilted for a 45 degree rip. With the gauge in the left table slot, place the first piece 'inside' down with top to the fence. Align the cut with the corner of the stock and clamp a stop onto the auxiliary fence. Cut the four sides in turn, then place the mitre gauge, without changing the angle into the right table slot. To cut the other side, flip the piece side to side ('inside' up) and end for end (bottom to fence). Re-position the stop and cut the four pieces.

The bottom is measured from the side pieces (which in this case should all be the same) and, with the blade now set for a five degree angle, cut the square bottom. Using a four-way clamp and shop made holding blocks, see page 125, dry assemble the sides and test the fit of the bottom piece. There are several brands of right angle assembly clamps available from suppliers. The holding blocks are nothing but scrap with dadoes perpendicular to each other and slightly wider than the thickness of the sides. Splines or biscuits are used to join the sides while screws hold the sides to the base. Though screws and glue could be used to join the sides, the base screws are covered by the plinth moulding. The profile of this moulding is unclear from the original illustration, but what is shown in the picture left will do nicely. While the table saw blade is set at five degrees, you can bevel the bottom edge of your moulding stock. The top of the plinth stock is formed with a round-over router bit.

Secure the sides in the work station, being careful of the delicate edges. Wait to carve the bottom V-groove and the top bead until after assembly so there are no problems with misalignment. The carving is in low relief ($^3/_{16}$ inches or 4$^1/_2$mm) similar to previous projects. Because the design extends nearly to the corner, you have to be extremely careful not to carve into the biscuit or spline holding the sides together. One solution is to slope the ground from the surface down to the depth of relief. Marking the depth of the biscuit slot on the top edge may help determine the slope. This does soften the 'frame' effect of the flat border. This also throws into question the use of stippling for the ground. Even stippling of the slope would be a tedious endeavour and might visually complicate the relationship of border to ground. (See also page 104.)

With relatively large areas of ground it may be difficult to ground evenly from one area to another, but it is important to strive for this outcome. A simple pencil depth gauge set to the desired depth will facilitate this process. By placing it on the surface the pencil will mark the high area. A router can be used to ground, but be mindful to allow for the sloping area of the ground.

Use a # 9 gouge to **bost** the areas between leaves and a #3 gouge to excavate and to

roughly ground. A #7 gouge used parallel to the border creates a good curve for the slope of the ground. Note that the vine 'sprouts' from the surrounding surface. Work the vine so that it has a smooth flow. You want to carve the general shape of leaves before detailing the leaflets. Small #5 or 7 gouges are good to set in these leaflets. After final modelling and grounding, a #15 run along the vines cleans and slightly undercuts them. The other elements can be slightly undercut but the shallow relief does not require it.

Above **Detail of the design**

Drill screw holes in the sides to hold the bottom piece and make sure they are adequately countersunk. Flip the sides over and lightly countersink the inside to make sure there are no burrs to interfere with a tight glue joint. Dry assemble to ensure that the pieces haven't warped during the carving process. I inserted the bottom piece, but did not glue it. The bottom piece has sloped sides and is sized to fit the narrow end of the box (see picture page 125). After the glue of the mitre joints cured, I glued and screwed the bottom in place. I then returned the waste basket to the bench to carve the V-groove and the bead. Lastly, I glued on the plinth pieces. Though I used penetrating oil on the exterior, I varnished the interior.

Example: Tray

Though trays might be considered the shallowest of bins and out of place in this chapter, they nonetheless have sides and bottom. In this case it is carved 'from the solid' and not assembled from pieces, but certainly low sided boxes are used for similar tasks. Rarely are trays lidded.

The tray in the picture at the top of page 129 has a design reminiscent of the Art Nouveau style popular a century ago. It was a liberating style which emphasized the organic, asymmetry and exuberance reminiscent of baroque, and rococo undulations and flamboyance. I have carved Art Nouveau trays previously and find this accessory is an easy way to experiment with the style. Art Nouveau often combines abstract shapes with literal or natural objects. Differing from the strict geometry of Celtic designs, the tray in the picture on page 129 consists simply of spaghetti-like tendrils.

The tray is two dimensional in concept but more sculptural than many of the other accessories in this book. The practical considerations are size, balance and practical use. Size determines use; a small tray such as the one demonstrated on this page can be used for a wine bottle and several glasses, for a loaf of ciabatta or for hor d'oeuvres. When held with two hands the tray should be balanced, so that there is no effort to keep the contents from falling. The tray should be made of a moderately hard wood for durability. The carving should not produce sharp projections nor deep recesses

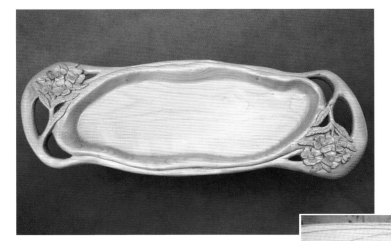

Above **Completed tray of primroses**

Right **Forstner bit used to waste interior of tray**

Right An Art Nouveau tray

Below An Art Nouveau
tray with whiplash tendrils

which might collect dust and debris. One half of this design has an asymmetrical curving silhouette which is rotated 180 degrees for the opposite end. The curving lines allow for some spaces to be cut through as well as an area for flowers, in this case the evening primrose (*Oenothera biennis*).

I chose the evening primrose because of its simplicity and suitability for the use of the tray, eschewing delicate petals which might be hard to clean or would chip off. The primrose has four 'generic' petals, but the stigma forms a noticeable X or cross shape. Around the perimeter are two abstract 'vines' which undulate. They could have been made less abstract with intertwining and additional leaves, though the primrose is an upright stalk plant and not a vine.

The blank for this tray should be made of a single piece of wood if possible as glue lines might be very distracting. This example is about 8½ inches (216mm) x 16 inches (406mm). Using a closed grain wood such as American black cherry allows for a nice finish. Though I have often pointed out that prominent grain patterns interfere with the forms of one's carvings, this project is one in which a little grain pattern might be desirable. First, there is a fairly large flat area which would do well to have something of interest and second, the organic curves re-enforce the idea of the Art Nouveau design. The grain pattern of the cherry is noticeable without crossing the (wavy) line to distraction. The material should be thick enough for the ends where the handles are to be above the table top so that it can be easily picked up. This example began with a blank 1½ inches (38mm) thick. To excavate the interior it is best to use a Forstner bit in a drill press. It is easy to drill a series of holes to the same depth using a drill press.

Above **Pencil guage used to obtain a uniform depth (and thickness of bottom)**

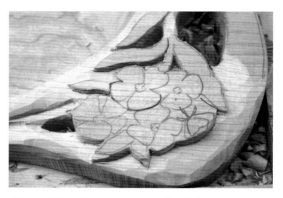

Above **The flowers are raised from background vines**

You can also use a handheld drill with spacer block to do this wasting. You can use a router, but the 1⅛ inches (28mm) that you want to remove requires multiple passes and a lot of dust besides. You can, of course, use gouge and mallet, but with this method you will have to be particularly careful as to the level and flatness of the bottom. For larger and less deep trays one can use a dado blade on a table saw, but this is potentially dangerous and not recommended. In that situation a router would be safer. For this size tray, I allowed ⅜ inch (10mm) thickness to remain, calculating that the tip of the Forstner bit would leave a small dimple below the surface and that the blank might distort and would require remediation later. The final thickness of the bottom would be ¼ inch (6mm) or so.

Jigsaw the piercings and band saw the silhouette. The band sawn blank might be difficult to secure because of its curved silhouette, so plan on using a work station or jig to hold it.

Using a fairly large #7 and smaller #3 slope the sides of the tray toward the bottom. This inner band can change slope though you also want to replicate the outline of your design. You also want to retain as much useable flat bottom as possible. Remember that the long sides will be undulating. Simultaneously, clean the ground with a broad #3. Using a #9 gouge at the base of the wall helps clean the corner. Be sure to carve enough of the bottom to erase any dimples made by the Forstner bit. A simple pencil gauge can indicate where the bottom needs to be levelled.

Begin lowering the sides. The area with the primroses and the handle are high.

The section through the handles should be thicker on the outside. Though there are some narrow trenches and small recesses among the leaves and flowers, the work is generally shallow. The flowers toward the outer edges are lowered so as not to be sticking out.

The back cutting is not only used for thinning the edge for aesthetic reasons, but also to form the exterior of the tray and to create the handles. A knife can be used to clean the acute angles of the piercing.

Cherry, being hard and closed grained, will show the minutest of scratches so it will need to be sanded with a succession of grits, finally

Left A variety of sanding aids. Cherry will need to be sanded with a succession of grits

using 600 grit paper. You should carve the piece as smoothly as possible before sanding. There is a plethora of gizmos to aid in the drudgery of sanding, from small drum sanders for drill or rotary tool, rubber forms, disks and flap sanders. Many shop-made forms can be inexpensively fabricated from scraps.

I have mentioned the use of varnish as an interior finish for the utensil boxes and the waste basket or planter above, but not advocating it for general woodcarving, believing that a dull sheen is better. The reflections from the surface created by shiny finishes distract the viewer, muddling the light and shadow of the form. But the practical necessity of having to clean a tray with soap and water requires a moisture resistant finish. Several coats of satin polyurethane will do. Because of the sculptural nature of this design there are no convenient break points in order to finish one side before completing the other side. I have found that instead of using a brush to apply the varnish, a number of coats wiped

on with a cotton cloth serve to allow for one side to be done first, blending the overlaps more easily and to create a duller finish. I lightly sanded a few places of build-up, and used non-woven abrasive (scotch) pads to buff the finish. A detail of the finished primrose is shown below.

Right Detail of finished primroses

The design of this small box is taken directly from one illustrated in Paul Hasluck's *Manual of Traditional Wood Carving*. It is a square 'handkerchief' box, and though I have modified the construction of the box slightly, I have followed the traditional form. The box is supported by a frame which is cut to create feet as well as a silhouetted apron. The lid with a simple shaped edge projects from the body of the box. The carved designs are the ever popular oak and laurel branches design illustrated. The oak, of course, stands for immortality and endurance; and the laurel is for renewal, resurrection, glory, honour, and, because it is evergreen, immortality. The box is personalized by a monogram in the centre of the lid. If you use a lock, as I did here, the placement of the keyhole must be anticipated when designing the front of the box.

Above **Jewellery box after Hasluck**

Right **The front design allowing for the keyhole**

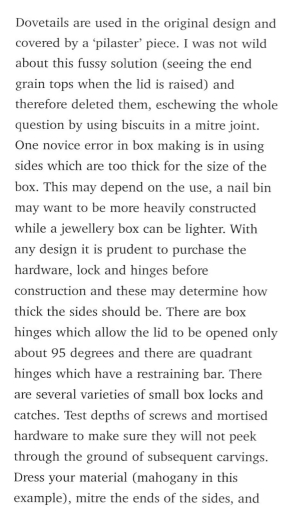

Above **The carving is quite shallow; showing routed ground, setting-in and modelling**

Above **The base underside showing back-cutting of apron silhouette**

Dovetails are used in the original design and covered by a 'pilaster' piece. I was not wild about this fussy solution (seeing the end grain tops when the lid is raised) and therefore deleted them, eschewing the whole question by using biscuits in a mitre joint. One novice error in box making is in using sides which are too thick for the size of the box. This may depend on the use, a nail bin may want to be more heavily constructed while a jewellery box can be lighter. With any design it is prudent to purchase the hardware, lock and hinges before construction and these may determine how thick the sides should be. There are box hinges which allow the lid to be opened only about 95 degrees and there are quadrant hinges which have a restraining bar. There are several varieties of small box locks and catches. Test depths of screws and mortised hardware to make sure they will not peek through the ground of subsequent carvings. Dress your material (mahogany in this example), mitre the ends of the sides, and

saw the rabbet to receive a 5mm plywood bottom. I used #0 biscuits, but a spline or a routed lock mitre joint could also be used. I used a four way frame clamp to dry assemble the box. Next, I installed the lock in order to locate the keyhole. I checked the design and altered it to accommodate a circular margin around the keyhole.

I carved the four sides. The depth of relief is only $1/16$ inch (1.5mm) so it may be more efficient to rout the ground with an $1/8$ inch (3mm) straight bit. The carving has some implied depth by having several leaf tips turned over, but again, because the depth is not great there is little need to undercut the elements. In the picture above left the stages of carving are shown with the routed blank at top, the set-in of the design outline and the modelled laurel leaves.

After gluing together the box, make and shape the apron or feet. First, saw the rabbet in which the box will rest; then place a saw kerf in the back of the stock to create a lip so that screws can hold the

Left **The top showing laurel, oak and monogram**

Below **Detail of top: oak leaves**

frame to the bottom of the box. Next, profile with router bits and block plane the ogee front. Final sanding can wait until after assembly. With scroll saw or fret saw, cut the silhouette along each side. Assemble with mitre joints. Mitre so that the box fits snuggly. The back of the frame is thinned with gouges and the holes for the screws are countersunk. Alternatively, you can assemble before routing the outer profile if you have a router table and sharp bit. Be careful of tear out at the corners.

The lid is a single piece of material and must be absolutely flat in order for the lock to engage the strike plate. Carve the lid design in a similar manner to the sides, though there can be more depth of relief, both because the lid is thicker and because it is more visible and the primary surface. The monogram in the centre circle can be 'drawn' with a parting tool when there is no effort to separate the letters with overlapping members. It is more effective, however, to make an effort at overlapping or entwining the letters. A monogram, after all, should be perceived as a unit as opposed to separate initials. In order to do this, the letters should be raised from the ground; the circular ground must be relieved with a slope from the circumference.

Example: CD Cabinet

It always seems that our CD collection is in a jumble; Mozart in the company of Dylan and the Dead or Albinoni rubbing shoulders with Dave Mathews, Wynton Marsalis tapping toes with The Lace City Singers. There are precarious towers of cases on the plastic racks we have. In making this cabinet I knew that it could only house a portion of the crowd, but at least the door would hide any shenanigans. A cabinet is a box with a lid oriented such that the lid is a door. This cabinet is not so much modelled on the ones produced by the Cincinnati carvers, but inspired by them. The wall hung cabinet in the picture on page 136 is a grand (towering!) statement with lots of different areas for displaying porcelain, and many surfaces and shapes to decorate. It is symmetrical in silhouette while asymmetric in decoration, having a high relief panel juxtaposed to deep voids. As with much of the amateur work from Cincinnati this piece seems to be a carver's sampler with many different carving techniques employed. There are simple geometric 'chip-carved' repeats, flat carved decorations on every rail and stile, there are shallow carved (sunken) rosettes and leaves, as well as the **alto-relievo** dogwood (*Cornus florida*) branch. The frieze board at the top is carved with classical acanthus moulding.

Right **CD storage cabinet**

Above **Hanging wall cabinet**

I decided, partly on personal preference, to make a desk top cabinet. The carving is for the most part surface decoration, with the exception of the door which features a **mezzo-relievo** wood lily (*Lilium phildelphicum*), similar to that depicted on the wall box on page 47. I hope the comparison of these two lily carvings illustrates again how technique improves with experience. The designs are not so different, but you'll notice an increased crispness, better depiction of depth, more delicate and delineated detail. The frame

of the lily seems to hang from a wall as the background is diapered, while the circular frame seems more like a window through which one sees branches of a tree reaching toward the sky.

The carcass is made with a divider so that two stacks of CDs can be enclosed. I bought four sets of plastic racks (from a hardware supply company) which are screwed to the interior sides and partition. The clearance is only five inches (127mm) so it makes sense

Left **Detail of the top**

Below **Detail of the lily carving**

to mount the racks before assembly. You could, of course, dado the sides to accept the CDs. Allow space top and bottom so the last CDs can be removed easily. I chip carved a simple repeat of squares (by carving two strings of triangles) down the edge of the middle partition.

The base is constructed in a similar way to the jewellery box previously described. I cut the silhouette and carved peacock, flowers, and plant in pie-shaped areas.

The configuration of the top is similar to Italian Renaissance cassone lids. It is also heavily influenced by Japanese furniture which, in turn, adds to the similarity to Aesthetic Movement style examples. The top piece with the flutes and surmounting pierced ornament is actually a lid for the space enclosed by the cornice. The door is hinged and held by a magnet and inlaid heart of steel.

"Since 'creativity' and 'mindfulness' may be two ways of looking at many of the same qualities of mind, there is no end to the parallels that could be made between the two."

Ellen J. Langer, *Mindfulness*

Chapter Six

Carving on Turnings

◆ **English Renaissance Candlestick** ◆ **Tripod Candlestick** ◆ **Paw-Footed Candlestick**
◆ **Santa Croce Lamp** ◆ **Tray**

Thus far, the carvings described in this book have been on flat surfaces with only a few exceptions. We now turn to accessories comprising blanks first turned on a lathe and then decorated; that is, designs for and techniques of carving curved surfaces.

Not all possible techniques are here discussed, but I have addressed several techniques in both my previous books where I discussed a layered rosette and a large pineapple finial.

The round form presents a continuous surface and like an effective sculpture, should draw the eye around it. Decorative carving, however, is applied to the form while sculpture is the form itself.

Even the flutes of the bowl in the picture below do not define the form but complement or accentuate it. Generally, decorative elements either circle the form, are oriented longitudinally along the axis, or there is (preferably) a combination of the two. Classically inspired urns, for instance, may have egg and dart or bead and billet mouldings around the form as well as a series of longitudinal flutes or upright leaves which circle the form.

There is something fascinating about the ancient art of woodturning, and it is often

Right **The flutes on this bowl serve to complement the form**

Left **Notice how the repeating elements are evenly distributed on this grape plate**

an end in itself, both practically and aesthetically. Here we are carrying the art of turning one step further by embellishing the form with decorative carving. The decoration on turnings can be more easily integrated with the form than with flat surfaces which often require borders or are confined by structural rails and stiles.

Rejuvenation

As with many crafts, such as quilt making, woodturning has experienced a widespread rejuvenation in the last few decades, and with it an expansion of both definition and practice. There are numerous artists carving

the turned form as well as combining disparate materials, various finishes and multiple processes, such as multi-axis turning and sawing and reassembling.

There are essentially two methods of turning; between centres, and faceplate turning. Refer to a good guide book such as *Wood Turning with Richard Raffan* for basic woodturning instruction. The candlestick shafts here are turned between centres while the tray is turned using a faceplate. Carving on turning presents some challenges. Layout of the various elements can be tricky because they need to fit accurately on the given circumference. Secondly, securing the blank requires special attention and ingenuity because it has to be firmly held yet periodically rotated. Leaving the blank on the lathe, locked in place by the indexing head or by wedges, is one possibility, but it is often prudent to fabricate a holding jig. One possibility is explained on page 155.

To begin with, the form of the blank should be pleasing before it is carved with ornamentation. For the most part, decorative carving on a turned form is surface, or **basso-relievo** technique and not sculptural carving. It is possible to attain high relief by turning and carving 'layers' which are then assembled. This process is explained in detail in my book *Carving Architectural Detail in Wood*. In designing for a turned form, the circumference of the blank is usually divided into even units, quarters and eighths, so the repeating elements are evenly distributed. Sometimes, of course, odd numbered units are used (see candlestick below), but even distribution, again, is necessary. The odd number of units will have 120 degrees for three units, 72 degrees for five units, and so on. Marking opposite sides of the turning at 180 degrees (or 90 degrees) will provide a starting point to estimate the odd unit placement which is then checked by 'walking' dividers around the form. This essential layout aids in locating both the circumferential and longitudinal elements. Even on a round flat surface, such as the plate with grapevine border pictured left, the tendency is to have

a repeating layout. As intimated above, some carved elements of a between centres turning will be perpendicular to the viewer while ones around the form will be distorted or only partially seen. Small repeating elements, such as beads (see page 160), enhance the urge to look around the form, while such elements on flat surfaces might appear static or monotonous.

Candlesticks

One of the primary design considerations for all candlesticks is stability. Stability is determined by two factors: the centre of mass (centre of gravity) and the ratio of effective base width to height. No doubt there are complicated formulas to determine these things, but it seems sufficient to make the base width at least a third of the height. Candles are relatively heavy (but get lighter as time burns on!). The candlesticks here are quite stable, consisting of a base, a shaft, a **bobeche** (or dish) containing a receptacle (cup or hole) for the candle.

Right **Candlesticks need to be stable**

These candlesticks are reminiscent of the woodwork of the English Renaissance; while unsophisticated in design, they have a bold and sturdy presence. They are straightforward with relatively simple elements and the execution of these elements is uncomplicated. Tool marks give it a painterly quality. The pierced carving of the base is similar to that of the Florentine frame in Chapter Four.

Referring to the drawing, prepare the blank for the top by drilling the hole in the stock. The candles for these candlesticks are 1½ inches (38mm) in diameter and 9 inches long (228mm). Square blanks are safer and easier to drill on a drill press because they can be secured against fences.

Allow the paddle bit to just project from the bottom as this will locate the centre during assembly. This does present a difficulty in mounting the piece to the lathe, so mount a scrap piece of wood to a faceplate and turn a plug (or spigot) with a shoulder so the drilled blank will be held without wobble as shown in the picture opposite.

An off-centre screw will prevent the blank from slipping on the spigot. Turn the profiles as shown on the drawing. The beads can be shaped by hand or with the assistance of a beading tool. The top is dished a little to catch any dripping wax.

Left English Renaissance candlesticks

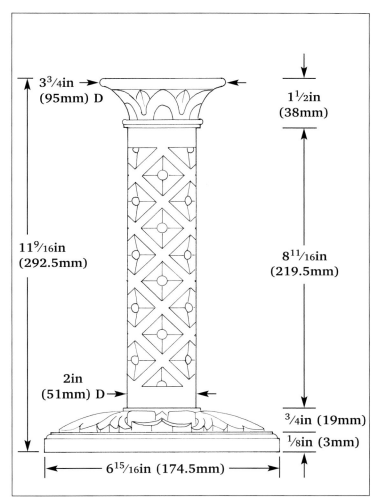

3³/₄in (95mm) D

1¹/₂in (38mm)

11⁹/₁₆in (292.5mm)

8¹¹/₁₆in (219.5mm)

2in (51mm) D

³/₄in (19mm)

¹/₈in (3mm)

6¹⁵/₁₆in (174.5mm)

Above **Drawing of the English Renaissance candlestick**

Lay out the design while the blank is still on the lathe, dividing the diameter into 32 divisions. It is easy to divide the circumference into quarters, then eighths, etc. If you do not have an indexing mechanism, using the tool rest as a starting point, you can 'walk' your dividers around the turning and by trial and error determine the quarters. Mark the upper extent of the points of the design and the placement of the small holes near the bottom bead. Sketch in the larger curves first, then the

Top right **Drilling the top for the candle**

Above **A turned spigot to hold the blank**

Left **The turned blank with turned beads**

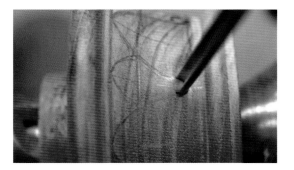

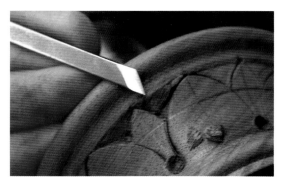

Left **Layout of top and setting in of eye**

Below left **The top leaves set-in**

smaller points between. Begin carving by stabbing in the small eyes with a #9 gouge, 4mm. Rotating the gouge between your hands will 'drill' the hole. Many plugs will pop out but those on end grain will need coaxing from the point of a 5mm skew or knife.

With a #7, 20mm gouge, stab in the large curves from the tip to the hole. Do the same for the smaller curves using a #5, 8mm gouge. Relieve the triangular areas between the points with a fishtail chisel or #3 fishtail. A skew chisel cleans out the acute corners. The ground should be perpendicular to the axis of the turning. Lower the small points by cutting toward the adjacent large points. Scoop a thumbnail depression at the base of the large points using #8, 10mm to complete the top.

The shaft should have parallel sides, facilitating the layout of the grid or diaper pattern. Mark 16 longitudinal lines using the tool rest as guide. Calculate four and one half divisions, allow for more margin at the bottom and spin the blank to mark circumference lines. Mark the centre circle of each square.

Above left **Clean between leaves with skew, relieve background leaves**

Left **Scoop the centre of leaves**

Right **Using flexible straight edge to layout diagonals**

Below right **Clamp the blank in a V-shaped cradle**

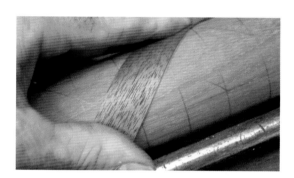

The picture top right shows a method for marking the diagonal lines using a flexible wood strip or veneer as a straight edge. Mark lines ether side of this diagonal grid to define the flat band between the sloping elements. If carving on the bench, a V-shaped 'cradle' will hold the cylinder while allowing it to be easily turned. Note the block for clamping at the left end.

To carve, set in the centre bead with a #9, 8mm. Then, using a chisel, slope the sides of the inverted pyramid beginning toward the bead and working out to the lines of the grid. Several settings-in of the circle will be required to obtain a depth at least half as wide as the circle. The two pictures on the bottom right show the sequence of cuts. Use the same #9 gouge, turned over, to round the beads. A #5, 8mm (or #7, 8mm) gouge will round the end half beads sufficiently.

For the carved base piece transfer the profile to the ends of the stock. On the table saw create the 'step' in the stock and cut off waste from the sloping profile. Hand plane

Above right **Using chisel to begin sloping pyramid to centre circle**

Right **Sequence of cuts**

Left **Rounding the centre bead with a #9 gouge**

Below left **Hand plane curved profile for base pieces**

the sloping profile. Mitre the four sides and join with biscuits or splines. Place the slots away from the curved (front) side of the stock so they are avoided while carving.

After glue-up make sure the top and bottom surfaces are flat. Use the carbon paper method to transfer the design of the corner leaves to the material.

Scroll or band saw the outer silhouette of leaflets and drill and cut the pierced holes.

To begin carving, lightly stab in the arcs of the scroll with the #7 gouges which match the curves.

Left **Base pieces showing biscuits and four-way or frame clamp**

Below left **Layout by the carbon paper method**

Below **The piercings cut out**

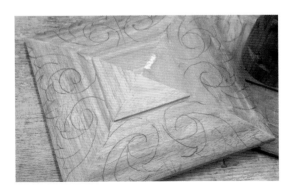

Above **Stab in the curves of the scrolls**

Below **Round the outside of the scroll at centre**

Above **Relieving cove of the scroll**

Relieve into the round part of the scroll both from the corner leaf direction and the centre element. Continue the relief around the centre of the scroll.

Further relieve the curve as it touches the raised square by removing material along the centre line of the centre leaf. The scroll slopes into a triangular hole. The fishtail chisel is helpful here.

The scroll arcs down the corner (along the mitre joint). This cut should also be sloped into a valley which dies about $\frac{1}{3}$ down the leaf toward the corner. Round over the 'eye' of the scroll with the #5, 8mm as in the picture below. Set in the

Above **Relieve toward corner**

Right **Round the eye of the scroll**

Left **Set-in the centre leaflets**

Below left **The lower leaflets of the corner are modelled**

flaring leaflets of the centre design to define their curve and to act as stop cuts so the back three leaflets of the corner leaf can be lowered.

The #7, 10mm is used to carve grooves down each leaflet. If necessary, make centre points symmetrical and visually compare the flaring leaflets. With larger #7 or #5 set in the sweep of the flaring leaflets to meet at the centre line. Take down the centre point by angled cuts either side with #5, 8mm creating a peak. Round the outside of the flares with the #5, then scoop out the inner side of the flares creating a curved peak from the centre line to the tip of the flared leaflet.

Remove the piece from the vice or work station and clamp it to the bench for access to the edges. With a #7, 8mm approaching from the edge, make sure the three inner leaflets of the corner leaf arc smoothly into the scroll. The thickness of the leaflets should be about $\frac{1}{16}$ of an inch. With the #9, 8mm gouge cut two grooves either side of the mitre to the leaflets, which breaks up the

Above left **Slope symmetrically the centre point**

Left **Round and model the flared leaflets of the centre element**

Above **Thin the lower leaves**

Above **Model the corner leaves**

Right **Finished corner leaf**

flat surface of the corner leaf. To finish, turn over and back cut around the holes. Then, using a knife, do any final shaping of leaflet tips and clean up the acute angles between them. The plain base piece has a routed quarter round moulding.

The pieces are glued and screwed together. The centre hole of the top lines up with the turning centre dimple of the shaft, and a centre hole in the base pieces lines up with the bottom dimple of the shaft. Screws directly in the centre should also have a second or third screw to prevent torque. The carved base is glued to the plain base before drilling the centre screw hole.

As for finish, Renaissance woodwork is usually very dark, so use walnut stain and then a paste wax or similar product to add a little sheen. Four cork or adhesive backed felt dots on the bottom protect the tabletop or mantelshelf surface. A square shaft version is illustrated in the picture right. The base is identical to the one just described, but the treatment of the shaft makes it more in the Aesthetic style.

Right **Square shaft version**

Above **Tripod candlestick complete**

Right **Renaissance example drawing**

This second candlestick has a tripod derived base, a baluster-like shaft and a metal bobeche and cup. The **tripod** is an ancient accessory used for a number of functions, but certainly among them is the torch. They were valued so much that they were given as prizes at poetic events in Ancient Greece. The configuration has reappeared throughout history. Tripods are easy to make and will stand without the possibility of rocking as a four legged table often does. Many candlesticks with this style of base make use of scrolls as the leg decoration, sometimes with classical acanthus foliage on the outside of the foot, similar to the scrolled bracket common in classical architecture. Different motifs are found in

the lateral concave curved section: shells, cherubs, lion heads as well as foliage and diaper patterns. The picture left shows an example from the Italian Renaissance.

This example is a simplified version!

There are several ways to construct the base blank: by assembling three pieces or by turning a solid block and then cutting the curve between the feet. It should be obvious that smaller bases can be fabricated by the second method while it is easier to construct larger bases with separate pieces.

The diameter of this base is 6½ inches (165mm) so you can turn the outside profile on the lathe. Though blanks may be difficult to mount accurately on the lathe, the neat thing is that you can easily true it by turning, just band saw the circular blank oversized. Recess the bottom, but leave the bottom of the feet slightly flat so that further operations are safe and true. To avoid any chance of the scrolls appearing flattened, however, some historical examples have the scrolls resting on balls, ovoids or paws, as in the picture on

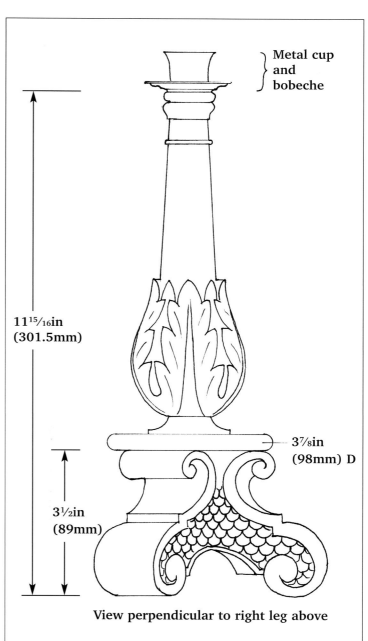

Metal cup and bobeche

$11^{15}/_{16}$in (301.5mm)

$3^{7}/_{8}$in (98mm) D

$3\frac{1}{2}$in (89mm)

View perpendicular to right leg above

Above **Drawing of tripod candlestick**

Left **Base turned on lathe**

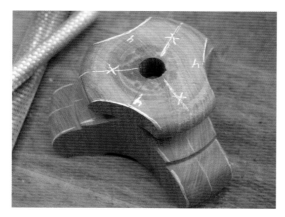

Above **The base divided into three legs**

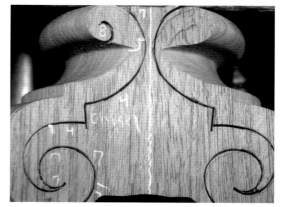

Above **Layout of the concave surface**

page 150. Lay out the legs 120 degrees apart on the top of the blank and draw the curves. After band sawing these curves, use files to smooth them.

Extend centre lines down these curves. Drill a hole in the top to receive the dowel end of the shaft.

To secure the blank, clamp it in a vice. Using the centre lines and a drawing of the scroll, transfer the curves to the interior extend of the scroll, the exterior being already determined by the turned blank.

To begin carving, set in the interior line of the scroll using sweeps which match the line. The picture above shows the sweep numbers adjacent to the layout lines. The spirals can be set in and relieved with several widths of the #7 sweep while other segments require a chisel, a #3 and for the top scroll, an #8 gouge.

Relieve the ground between the scrolls, maintaining the curve of the original surface. The vertical surface should remain parallel to the axis of the turning.

Below **Relieve the top scroll with a deep gouge**

Below **The scroll is relieved and internal area grounded**

Left **The lower arch is shaped**

Below **The scale diaper**

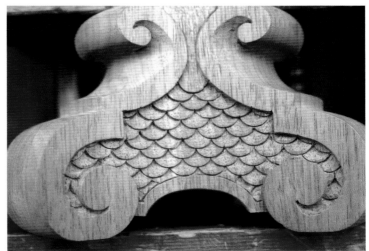

Draw the centre curve at the bottom on the
three concave sides, see picture above, and
cut them with appropriate gouges.

Re-position the blank so the bottom can be
cleaned up from the previous operation and
dish the middle slightly. Return to the
original vice position and draw the border to
this arch. The scale diaper, like its use on the
bookends of Chapter Three, breaks up the
flat curved surface and also presents contrast
to the undecorated outer surfaces of the feet.

The width of the legs could be narrowed
somewhat, or decorated with foliage as
mentioned or a moulding profile typical of
many scrolled brackets consisting of centre
astragal and flanking cyma curves.

The shaft is a straightforward turning.
The bottom end has a dowel so it can be
inserted into the base. The bulge is carved
with generic foliage (see picture right)
while still on the lathe though a pillow
block jig, as explained on page 155, could
be used. The metal cup and bobeche can
be ordered from woodworking or hobby
supply houses. The two pieces are simply
screwed to the top of the candlestick.

Above **Generic foliage is carved on the shaft**

More prevalent in Roman candlestands is a variation of the tripod by the use of three paw feet peeking out from the turned base. The shaft here is a classical baluster, with leaves sprouting from a centre beading. The three-armed top is drilled for three regular candles and finished with brass collars available from supply houses. In similar fashion to the previous candlestick, this one was made from parts and assembled. Soft maple (*Acer rubrum*) was the wood used. The base and shaft, or baluster, are turned, the latter with dowels at both ends.

The mouldings or forms are simple ones; the **cavetto** of the base and the curves of the baluster. Turn the baluster with dowel ends to fit snuggly in the holes of top and base. This baluster has a top which flares out to a wide fillet to support the top, while the bottom rests directly on the round flat of the base. The top piece is a flat board with a hole on the underside for the shaft dowel. The quarter round moulding on the

Above **The paw-footed candlestick**

Right **The base is secured in the work station**

underside of the top is made with router and round-over bit. The **gadrooning** of the base is geometrically laid out. I originally divided the circumference into 16 parts, as it is easy from diameter, perpendiculars, 45 degrees and then 22.5 degrees, but the bulbous ends would look too wide, I reasoned. I divided the circumference into 18 units of 20 degree angles. Hold the blank in a circular recess jig or jammed into a corner of the work station, see the picture below left.

The challenge to this carving is the constantly changing direction of the grain. Run a valley with the parting tool along the layout lines and then deepen the valleys while rounding over the gadroon with a #5 gouge turned over. Several sizes are used as the round diminishes in diameter. After working around the circle, the ends need to be rounded and a #7 gouge stabbed down will probably accomplish this as they are not semicircles but arcs. A mallet may be required, but be careful not to mar the ground which is created perpendicular to the cavetto (the small step turned to separate the cavetto from the gadroon). Though one should carve as smoothly as possible, some sanding in this instance is necessary.

It doesn't matter what is carved next: baluster or paw feet. If you are not going to carve the baluster on the lathe, the best way to hold the blank is by the dowel ends resting in pillow blocks. Simply drill a hole the same size as the dowel ends in two scrap blocks, then cut them in half through the

hole. Mount one half of each block on a base of plywood the length of the baluster apart so the dowel ends rest in the grooves. Screw the tops onto the bottoms, the material wasted by the saw kerf allows the two halves to pinch the dowel ends.

You could also hold the baluster in a jig consisting of a length of stock with a V cut into the length as we did for the English Renaissance candlestick. The baluster is not large enough in circumference to carve four leaves comfortably. Three leaves might be considered more appropriate anyway, echoing the three paw feet.

I usually advocate working out design problems on paper before work begins, but it is time-consuming to figure the spacing of the convex/concave shape of the turned blank. Divide the circumference of the blank into six even divisions.

Below **Pillow blocks hold the shaft securely**

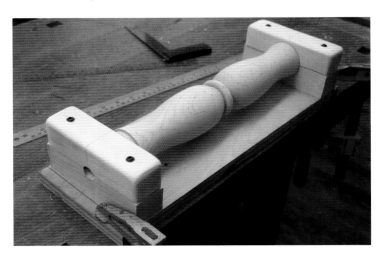

Above **Using the tracing paper method of design transfer**

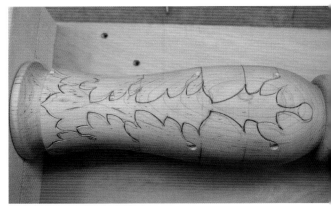

Above **The completed transfer and background leaf added**

Three will represent the centre of the three leaves. The other three divisions represent the extent or width of the leaves (with a little space between them). A quick sketch on paper of a leaf of the required length may be helpful, but end up sketching the leaf directly on the blank making sure it fits the space. In fact, it may be prudent to hold the leaflet tips back slightly from the dividing line so the ground can later be excavated more easily. When satisfied, trace one half of the leaf and use the tracing to transfer the design to the other spaces, flipping it over when required. Your patience will be tried in keeping the

flimsy tracing paper properly aligned. A snip in the edge will allow the pattern to be held in the concave part of the turning. It must be said that the leaves on either side of the centre beading do not necessarily have to line up, but could be off-set by 60 degrees. According to classical precedent for balance and symmetry, they should be lined up as here presented. At the ends of the baluster, the space left by the diminishing leaf tip should be filled in with a leaf tip which rises from behind the three main leaves. This is a dummy or background leaf which 'fades' into the ground. This ground should not be stippled. As with the previous leaves, the

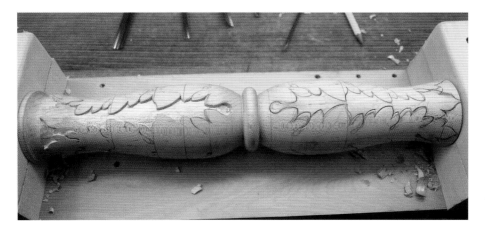

Left **The area between leaves is grounded**

Left **Model the leaves**

Right **Carving the beads**

leaf tips should be set-in and the space between them grounded. The leaflets are then stabbed in, including the eye, and the ground between the three primary leaves lowered so that it is about an ¹/₈ inch (3mm) below the original turned surface.

If you have done this consistently, the ground echoes the curve of the original surface. With the parting tool define the centre vein, relieving either side so that it stands above the surrounding leaf surface which is, of course, not hard to do on a curve! Finally, round over the vein.

Now turn to the modelling of the leaves. Relieve the leaflet which is overlapped, then, using several widths of #7s, groove the leaflets in long arcs originating from the centre vein.

It is hard to get a nice smooth flow on the convex shape, so some re-working might be necessary. The widths of #7s should be selected so they extend to the edges of the leaf. That is, nearly the entire width of the leaf should be slightly concave. The wider main leaflets may want to have a deeper middle made with a #8 gouge. Sink the eyes fairly deeply. They should be teardrop shaped and punches of this shape can be used after the waste is popped out to further define them. The turned centre bead can be left plain or subdivided into carved beads.

The paw feet are stylized lion's feet, common to this style stanchion. On many tripod braziers hoofed feet are also common, but rarely are eagle talons clutching a ball, so prevalent in eighteenth century furniture, found in historical examples. Using them would not be out of character, however.

To carve the paw feet, dimension the stock and band saw the side profile, as shown in the picture on page 158. The waste cut off can be used as a spacer as one carves the

Above **Blanks for the paws**

Below **Roughing the paw**

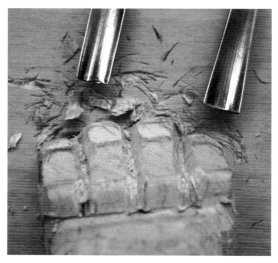

paw. Drill and countersink the screw holes. Clamp the blank with a C-clamp to the bench with a scrap piece of wood between. Round the sides and front of the leg and thin the ankle. Then shorten the length of the outside toes, rounding all four. The outside toes are lowered as well. Carve a valley to separate the toes; the knuckles bulge while the straight sections between are slightly concave.

Where the middle toes join the leg the crease should be rounded with a #9 or #11 to remove band saw marks. Remove the clamp and, using a knife, carve the outside knuckles and round the underside of the blank where it goes under the base of the candlestick. Placing the blank in a vice, set-in the claws using a small #9 and #5 to make a teardrop shaped claw.

Relieve around the claw and round the toe to the bottom of the blank. A relieving cut at the top of the claw will give it more presence.

Re-clamp on the bench and add the fur with a parting tool. A larger parting tool is used to provide some deep valleys and a smaller one for the overall texture.

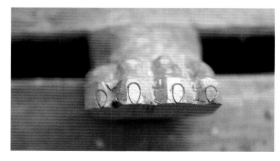

Above **The claws are set-in**

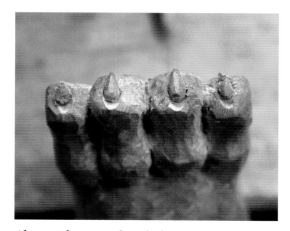

Above **The completed claws**

Example: Santa Croce Lamp

The design for the lamp here is taken from an illustration of a fountain base said to have been in the church of Santa Croce in Florence. I do not know if this fountain still exists, but it is a typical Renaissance design. I carved a candlestick replicating (more or less!) the middle 'column' of this fountain many years ago, see the picture on the top of page 160, and reprise it now as an electric lamp. The following discussion is aimed at providing the reader with a critique of the original and strategies I used to improve the quality of the second rendition.

Above **Lamp redux complete**

Left **Drawing of the fountain**

Left **Original candlestick**

Below **Lamp comparison**

Below right **Guilloche of original candlestick**

Bottom right **Lamp guilloche and acanthus leaves**

Whether one undertakes formal training or is self-taught, it is always instructive to look back over one's career and realize the evolution of one's skills and artistic sensibility. Creativity implies change, discovery, experimentation, 'pushing the envelope'. Retrospective exhibitions of an artist's work serve this purpose in a public way. They are helpful to note variety and change, but also to understand process. Part of that process is improvement. The same themes may dominate the body of work, but it may be the technique expressing those themes which has evolved or, conversely, the technique may remain essentially the same while the design, subject matter, or context changes. Often artists return to their early

Above **Egg and dart, waterleaf of original**　　　*Above* **New egg and dart**

work for its apparent felicity, freedom, youthful energy or simply to improve on it. In my original effort, all the hallmarks of ornamental naiveté are evident. Though the overall proportions may be satisfactory, the effect is heavy, though this may be necessary to hold up a marble fountain! Compare the pictures on the left. From bottom to top, the lower profiles are not the classical cyma or S-curved mouldings that they should be.

The guilloche around the neck (see picture left) lacks the circular geometry of the classical motif. The beads are technically awkward with small facets which don't reflect the light evenly. Compare with the picture bottom left. The acanthus leaves of the original are stiff and lack flow and are not of sufficient relief to allow the leaf to exist apart from the underlying form. They have a pasted on look. The flutes are very shallow and the egg and dart lacks the dart! The waterleaf is an abstract pattern here as opposed to a traditional stylized leaf. Compare the two

pictures above. The goal in this new version is to tweak the design somewhat, but primarily to execute the designs with better technique. I have carved all of these elements numerous times in the interim on a variety of objects. The design of this rendition appears more delicate even though the lamp is somewhat larger and this is achieved by more separate elements – more leaflets on the acanthus, deeper flutes and so forth. The crisper technique with somewhat more relief also contributes to this feeling.

I was also more faithful to the illustration by filling the spaces between the four acanthus leaves with a 'stiff' leaf, thus eliminating the blank look to the original urn-shaped turning.

Because this will be an electric lamp, accommodation for the wire has to be made. Grooving the two middle planks in the glue-up will allow the hollow lamp rod to extend through the blank at assembly. Temporary

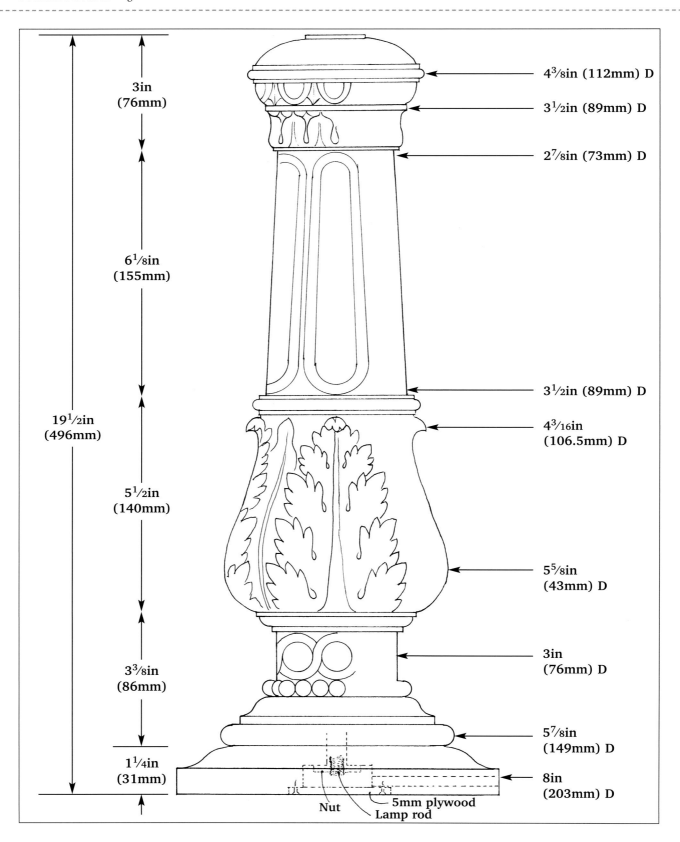

3in
(76mm)

4³⁄₈in (112mm) D

3¹⁄₂in (89mm) D

2⁷⁄₈in (73mm) D

6¹⁄₈in
(155mm)

3¹⁄₂in (89mm) D

4³⁄₁₆in
(106.5mm) D

19¹⁄₂in
(496mm)

5¹⁄₂in
(140mm)

5⁵⁄₈in
(43mm) D

3in
(76mm) D

3³⁄₈in
(86mm)

5⁷⁄₈in
(149mm) D

1¹⁄₄in
(31mm)

8in
(203mm) D

Nut

5mm plywood

Lamp rod

plugs in these square holes will allow mounting to the lathe. Making the large diameter base separately prevents the otherwise delicate vertical grain from being broken off. This also makes better use of material, avoiding a large glued up block. Though larger proportionally than the first version, the base provides weight and stability for the lamp and shade. It also provides visual stability as plain (unornamented) surfaces appear more formidable. There is a logical breakpoint between the cyma profile of the base and the large bead, allowing for a seamless design integration. To accommodate the

electric wire, a lateral hole should be drilled while the base blank still has parallel sides from glue-up (or the dressed edges of a solid piece). This makes it possible to use a drill press to drill a small hole to the centre of the laid-out circle.

The blank then is band sawn and screwed to a faceplate. After truing-up, recess a 3 inch (76mm) hole so that the threaded lamp rod with a nut, as well as the wire, can be accommodated. A stepped recess outside this hole allows for a thin plywood cover plate.

The carving procedure is similar to the previously described candlesticks. The flutes are semicircular in section and there is a surprisingly easy method to ensure this. The Theorem of Thales (Thales of Miletus, lived around 585 BC) states that an angle inscribed in a semicircle is a right angle. Therefore, a triangle whose base is the diameter of a circle and contained in a semicircle will comprise a 90 degree angle regardless of where the angle touches the semicircle. A small scrap of wood with a 90 degree corner can serve as a template or gauge. The sum of the angles of a triangle is 180 degrees, so the other angles increase and decrease as the 90 degree corner of the template is rotated around the interior of the flute. The diameter or base of the triangle is, of course, the width of the flute, so the template can be used at any point along the tapering flute. If there is space at one side of the template allowing the 90 degree corner to rock on the bottom of the flute, then more

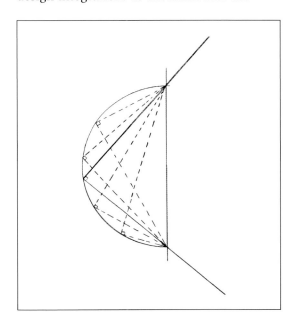

Above **Drawing of Theorem of Thales**

Left **Drawing of the new lamp**

Left **Use of a template to determine semicircularity of flute**

material has to be removed. If there is space underneath the 90 degree corner while the sides of the template are touching the width of the flute, then the flute is elliptical and a little too deep.

How did I improve technique, you may ask. The flippant answer, of course, is 'experience'. Better familiarity with historical precedent through study is the primary explanation. Developing an eye for which tool is to be used in a given situation has also contributed.

Most times there is an exact match between tool sweep and the intended cut. Even as you understand the overlap of sweeps there is one tool for optimum effectiveness. In roughing-out or in heavy excavation this is not so important, but you want to eliminate lots of facets on the finished surface. Light reflecting from each facet creates a visually complicated piece. Long sweeping cuts made in one pass are

ideal, therefore. If repeated setting-in is necessary, you should attempt to have a smooth vertical wall. Of course, subsequent undercutting will take care of some raggedness. Many amateurs are a little timid and do not create enough depth, so generally, when in doubt, go deeper. If you have planned well and visualize the form of the elements you shouldn't have to rework the surface too much (sure, we all have a hard time resisting the urge to revise). One important technique for good work is to stand back and evaluate; turn the work upside-down, turn off the lights, view it at a slant. And lastly, don't hurry. The more masterful you are, the more deliberate. This advice is probably reminding you of the introductory essay about efficiency. Efficiency, though workplace studies have given the concept a bad name, is a balance between concentration and evaluation.

Example: Tray

Left **This tray is carved with a flowing, profusion of detail**

Much carving on turning is simply carving a relief in a circle such as illustrated in the picture on page 140. Trays, stool seats and breadboards are a few examples. The tray described here is such a piece. The concept is derived from the eighteenth century piecrust table top and specifically such a table in the collection of the Museum of Southern Decorative Arts, Old Salem, North Carolina. The table 'piecrust' consists of C scrolls separating two symmetrical S scrolls with a foliage fan shaped spray between them. I have carried the idea just a little further in adding some leaflets to the scrolls.

Those table tops were turned with a broad rim raised from the surface. This rim, though given a profile on the inside edge, is then cut in silhouette and carved to extend the profile around the undulations of the silhouetted edge. This tray is similar in that the edge is cut in silhouette and the raised rim is carved, but instead of the rigid geometry of the traditional piecrust top, this one has more flow and a profusion of detail. There are some echoes of the piecrust in the secondary level, but the foliage scrolls and the fleur-de-lis shape are more prominent. Though grain matching doesn't usually have much influence, it does here because of the broad expanse of uncarved surface. The originals used one wide mahogany board. I oriented the four fleur-de-lis, being the dominant element, 45 degrees from the grain direction to de-emphasize them. Being 21 inches (525mm) in diameter, this tray could be made into a small tripod table typical of the eighteenth century. One difference, however, is the need for a substantial under cutting of the tray edge so that it can be picked up from a flat surface.

If the blank is glued up carefully so that any grain mismatch is not a distraction, wide boards are not necessary. They can be found from some suppliers, but one could argue that glued boards are in fact more stable. Band saw the board larger than the intended tray as mounting to the faceplate is seldom perfectly accurate. Attach a waste board to the back side of the blank. The

Above **The use of a straight edge and drafting triangle for quadrant layout**

Right **Double ended thickness caliper**

Left **Roughed – in ground**

Right **The upper level is separated from slope**

diluted glue and paper method often used in this situation might add a lot of moisture to one side of the blank, causing undue warp. Make sure you have a secure joint as UFOs are not welcome! With a table top which has underpinning mechanism ('bird cage') screw holes in the back surface might be acceptable, but not on a tray. Mount the faceplate to this scrap and onto the lathe.

True the circumference and reduce the blank to the desired diameter. Then true the flat face. Excavate the centre of the blank leaving the rim wide enough to include the carving. The depth allowed for the carving is ½ inch (13mm). Also, leave a column around the centre point which will serve as a reference point in the layout of the four repeats of the design. A double-ended caliper will allow you to determine the thickness of the tray surface. Leave it a little thicker than final intention so that warp can be corrected. There really isn't any profile to turn so lay out the various divisions using a straight edge and drafting triangle. A little

Right **The completed carving**

relief on the bottom side will furnish a reference for later back-cutting. Take the blank from the lathe and transfer the design previously drawn onto the flat rim. It is efficient to use a router with a straight bit to waste the inner material to obtain an approximation of the outline. Band saw the exterior silhouette.

Screw a scrap piece of plywood to the back block such that this base can be clamped to the bench top. Several scrap pieces are wedged between the base and the underside of the tray blank so that carving pressure doesn't pop the glue joints or split the wood. You may actually want to clamp from the top of the blank. The previously roughed-in outline and silhouette are cleaned up and made to

conform to the layout. The primary design elements are set-in by the usual stab and relieve method to a depth of ⅛ inch (3mm). The secondary connections are lowered an additional ⅛ inch. The primary elements are modelled and rounded. The slight cove which slopes down to the tray surface are carved with a chisel and a #3 gouge, commencing at the raised elements and

Below **Detail of the tray**

Above **Detail of the finished tray**

stopping $\frac{1}{16}$ inch (1.5mm) from the tray surface, leaving a slight vertical wall. You may need to work the ground in order to remove turning marks or to even the routed areas with the turned surface. Use a scraper to smooth the tray surface, then sand as desired.

After the top is completed, remove the base and the waste block and smooth the bottom which may have warped slightly. Turn the tray over onto a soft, padded surface and back-cut the edge rounding and echoing the front side profiles where appropriate.

As with the Art Nouveau tray of the preceding chapter, this tray will want to have a water resistant finish. I would, therefore, use a number of coats of satin varnish finish, well rubbed with steel wool. Pictured above and on p167 are details of the two elements.

Conclusion

The numerous woodcarving clubs and shows attest to the widespread interest in the art. Peruse any woodworking magazine and you will probably note some article which involves carving; certainly an announcement of a class or exhibition of carved work. This popularity is in conjunction with the larger cultural awareness of craft work whether quilting, scrapbooking, beading, porcelain painting or mosaic. There is a not-so-surprising adaptation of new technologies. Simultaneously, there is a revival of older crafts and historically based methods.

The craft interest of the nineteenth and twentieth centuries is, for the most part, dominated by the amateur. Though professional woodcarvers write books and assist the novice, the amateur is essential in preserving the cultural appreciation of the craft. For a number of reasons the professional woodcarver would find it difficult to earn a living producing the unique items presented in this book.

In a world which seems more impersonal despite the global village notion, the joys of handwork and the accompanying sense of accomplishment have no substitute. It is hoped that this book has provided a spark of inspiration, some firm guidance and contributed to your quality of life.

Glossary

Alto-relievo A relief carving in which approximately ¾ or more of the thickness of the subject is depicted.

Arris A corner, where two planes meet at an angle.

Backcutting A technique of removing material from the backside of a carving (usually a pierced carving) to reduce its apparent thickness.

Basso-relievo A relief carving of minimal depth.

Bobeche The dish at the top of a candlestick to catch dripping wax.

Bost/bost-in The process of roughly shaping a carving.

Cannel/in-cannel The name given to designate the concave side of a carving gouge.

Cavetto A concave moulding profile, more or less elliptical in section; a cove is a quarter round in section.

Cyma The double or S curve associated with classical moulding profiles.

Diaper A repeating pattern over a surface, 'wallpaper,' often on a grid system.

Edge Treatments Decorative repeats carved on one surface at a corner or edge.

Flat carving A type of relief where the elements are delineated by a shallow ground, with little or no surface modelling.

Gadrooning A series of lobe-like shapes, each usually narrower at one end so are teardrop shaped.

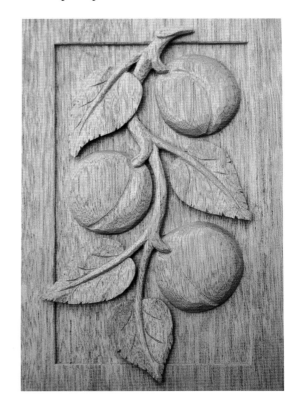

Top **Alto-relievo**

Right **Basso-relievo**

Ground The background of a relief carving. To ground is to lower a surface evenly.

Imbrication A surface carved such that the elements appear to overlap each other as in roof tiles or scales.

Incised carving The technique of 'drawing' in the wood with V-shaped lines.

Isometric view The graphic depiction of an object where two sides and top are presented equally.

Mezzo-relievo A relief carving of moderate depth, approximately ½ of the object is depicted.

Model The technique of carving the surface to show the object with more depth and/or realism, to make the surface three dimensional.

Negative space The voids or spaces between the solid (positive) areas of a carving.

Perspective The perception that objects further from the eye are smaller and how this phenomenon is represented pictorially.

Relieve The technique of removing wood in order to define an outline (and thus making a projection) as in 'stab and relieve' technique or removing wood in order to accentuate the object carved.

Sight edge Inner edge of a picture frame.

Set-in The technique of defining a shape or line of a design by stabbing perpendicularly to the surface of the wood, usually with the intention of creating a wall so the enclosed area is in relief.

Tripod A three legged (or footed) stanchion or support.

Undercutting The technique of relieving the underside or back side of the object being carved to make it appear separate from the ground.

About the Author

For thirty years Frederick Wilbur has been a professional woodcarver, specializing in traditional decorative carving for domestic, public and ecclesiastical architecture. He works with pipe organ builders, architects, millwork and furniture companies, and decorative arts designers. He has received the Architectural Woodwork Institute's Award of Excellence, and has videotaped a demonstration as part of the permanent exhibition of art-carved furniture at the Cincinnati Art Museum.

He lives and works with his wife, Elizabeth, in the Blue Ridge Mountains of central Virginia. They delight in their three grandchildren.

Credits: The music cabinet (page 11) is courtesy of the Cincinnati Art Museum, museum purchased funds provided by the Fleischmann Foundation in memory of Julius Fleischmann. The nineteenth century wall pocket (page 48) by a Cincinnati amateur carver is courtesy of the Cincinnati Art Museum, gift of Marguerite Nassauer. The frame showing classical elements (page 85) is courtesy of Martha Wilbur. The Renaissance frame and Baroque frame (page 86) are courtesy of Dover Publications Inc. The hanging wall cabinet (page 136) is courtesy of the Cincinnati Art Museum, gift of Walter E. Langsam in memory of his parents, Walter C. and Julia E. Langsam. The Renaissance example drawing (page 150) is courtesy of Dover Publications Inc. The fountain drawing (page 159) is courtesy of Dover Publications Inc.

Bibliography

In the middle of the nineteenth century, as industrialization began to displace the artisan woodcarver, and because more people had an interest in the arts and crafts, a large number of carving manuals for the amateur was published. Many of these books have recently been reprinted and are interesting on a number of levels. Original publication dates are in parentheses.

Hasluck, Paul N. (ed.) *Manual of Traditional Wood Carving*. Mineola, NY: Dover Publications, Inc. (1911) 1971.

Hodgson, Fred T. *Hodgson's Art of Wood Carving*. Ottawa: Algrove Publishing Limited, (1905) 2000.

Jack, George. *Wood Carving: Design and Workmanship*. London: Pittman, (1903) 1978.

Rowe, Eleanor. *Practical Woodcarving: Elementary and Advanced*. Mineola, NY: Dover Publications, Inc. (1907) 2005.

Wheeler, William and Hayward, Charles. *Woodcarving*. New York: Drake, 1976.

Several books might help elucidate the complex art movements, aesthetic theories and social preferences of the nineteenth century.

Atterbury, Paul and Wainwright, Clive. *Pugin: A Gothic Passion*. New Haven: Yale University Press (in association with the Victoria and Albert Museum), 1994.

Brolin, Brent C. *Architectural Ornament: Banishment and Return*. New York: Norton, 2000.

Flores, Carol A. Hrvol. *Owen Jones: Design, Ornament, Architecture and Theory in an Age in Transition*. NYC: Rizzoli International Publishing, Inc., 2006.

Jones, Owen. *The Grammar of Ornament*. London: Dorling Kindersley Books, 2001.

Rosenberg, John D. ed. *The Genius of John Ruskin*. Charlottesville, VA: University of Virginia Press, 1998.

Other works consulted (including historic design books):

Arenski, Jay; Daniels, Simon; Daniels, Michael. *Swiss Carvings: The Art of the 'Black Forest" 1820-1940*. Woodbridge, Suffolk, UK: Antique Collector's Club, Ltd., 2005.

Aslin, Elizabeth. *The Aesthetic Movement*. NYC: Excalibur Books, 1969.

Butler, Robert L. *Wood for Wood-carvers and Craftsmen: Source, Selection, Cutting, Treatment, Drying of Flitches, and Guidance in their Use*. New York, A.S. Barnes & Co., 1974.

Cole, Rex Vicat. *Perspective For Artists*. Mineola, NY: Dover Publications, Inc., 1976.

Esterly, David. *Grinling Gibbons and the Art of Carving*. London: V&A Publications, 1998.

Griesbach, C. B. *Historic Ornament: A Pictorial Archive*, Mineola, NY: Dover Publications, Inc., 1975.

Heydenryk, Henry. *The Art and History of Frames: An Inquiry into the Enchantment of Paintings*. New York: Lyons and Burford, 1963.

Hoadley, R. Bruce. *Understanding Wood: A Craftsman's Guide to Wood Technology*. Newtown, CT: Taunton Press, 2000.

Howe, Jennifer L. (ed). *Cincinnati Art – Carved Furniture and Interiors*, Athens, OH: Ohio University Press, 2003.

Krenov, James. *The Fine Art of Cabinetmaking*. New York: Van Nostrand Reinhold Co., 1977.

Lambourne, Lionel. *The Aesthetic Movement*. London: Phaidon Press, Ltd. 1996.

Lee, Leonard. *The Complete Guide to Sharpening*. Newtown, CT: Taunton Press, 1995.

Loy, Susan. *Flowers, the Angel's Alphabet*. Moneta, VA: CSL Press, 2001.

Meyer, Franz Sales. *Handbook of Ornament*, Mineola, NY: Dover Publications, Inc., 1957.

Morley, John. *The History of Furniture: Twenty-five Centuries of Style and Design in the Western Tradition*. Boston: Little, Brown, 1999.

Onians, Dick, *Essential Woodcarving Techniques*. Lewes, East Sussex: GMC Publications, 1997

Porter, Terry. *Wood Identification and Use*. Lewes, East Sussex: GMC Publications Ltd, 2004.

Pye, Chris, *Woodcarving Tools, Material and Equipment*, new edition in two vols. Lewes, East Sussex: GMC Publications, 2002.

Raffan, Richard. *Turning Wood with Richard Raffan*, Newtown, CT: Taunton Press, 1985.

Rettelbusch, Ernst. *Handbook of Historic Ornament*. Mineola, NY: Dover Publications, Inc., 1996 (originally published in 1937).

Simon, Jacob. *The Art of the Picture Frame: Artist, Patrons, the Framing of Portraits in Britain*. London: National Portrait Gallery, 1996

Spletz, Alexander. *The Styles of Ornament*. Mineola, NY: Dover Publications, Inc., (1910).

Stowe, Doug. *Taunton's Complete Illustrated Guide to Box Making*, Newtown, CT: Taunton Press, 2004.

Wilk, Chistopher. *Western Furniture: 1350 to the present day – in the Victoria & Albert Museum, London*. London: Cross River Press, 1996.

Metric Conversion Table

inches to millimetres and centimetres
mm = millimetres cm = centimetres

inches	mm	cm	inches	cm	inches	cm
⅛	3	0.3	9	22.9	30	76.2
¼	6	0.6	10	25.4	31	78.7
⅜	10	1.0	11	27.9	32	81.3
½	13	1.3	12	30.5	33	83.8
⅝	16	1.6	13	33.0	34	86.4
¾	19	1.9	14	35.6	35	88.9
⅞	22	2.2	15	38.1	36	91.4
1	25	2.5	16	40.6	37	94.0
1¼	32	3.2	17	43.2	38	96.5
1½	38	3.8	18	45.7	39	99.1
1¾	44	4.4	19	48.3	40	101.6
2	51	5.1	20	50.8	41	104.1
2½	64	6.4	21	53.3	42	106.7
3	76	7.6	22	55.9	43	109.2
3½	89	8.9	23	58.4	44	111.8
4	102	10.2	24	61.0	45	114.3
4½	114	11.4	25	63.5	46	116.8
5	127	12.7	26	66.0	47	119.4
6	152	15.2	27	68.6	48	121.9
7	178	17.8	28	71.1	49	124.5
8	203	20.3	29	73.7	50	127.0

Index

Guild of Master Craftsman Publications Ltd,

Castle Place, 166 High Street, Lewes, East Sussex BN7 1XU, United Kingdom

Tel: 01273 488005   Fax: 01273 402866   Email: pubs@the gmcgroup.com   Website:www.gmcbooks.com

Ask us for a complete catalogue or visit our website. Orders by credit card are accepted.